T0131806

GREAT GRAVES

of Upstate New York

CHUCK D'IMPERIO

iUniverse, Inc.
New York   Bloomington

Great Graves of Upstate New York

Copyright © 2007, 2008 by Chuck D'Imperio

iUniverse Star
an iUniverse, Inc. imprint

iUniverse books may be ordered through booksellers or by contacting:

iUniverse
1663 Liberty Drive
Bloomington, IN 47403
www.iuniverse.com
1-800-Authors (1-800-288-4677)

ISBN: 978-1-935-27830-6(pbk)
ISBN: 978-1-935-27831-3 (ebk)

Printed in the United States of America

iUniverse Rev. Date: 12/24/2008

This book is dedicated to Louis A. D'Imperio and Joseph A. Cody. The Italian shoemaker and the Irish cop. They are my grandfathers. They are also my greatest legends.

ACKNOWLEDGMENTS

I started writing *Great Graves of Upstate New York* long before the time of a computer in every home. There was no Internet then, and most of my information came from good old-fashioned hard work. I traveled hundreds of miles researching these graves and discovering the many stories within the pages of this book. And what a wonderful education it has been for me. First and foremost, I would like to acknowledge and give a giant tip of the hat to all of the unknown and unnamed cemetery workers who helped me find these graves. They know who they are, and they were all wonderful. From the front desk office workers to the maintenance crews who keep our state's cemeteries so beautiful, I say a big thank you for all of your help. Many times I think these people were surprised when I happened along and actually took interest in what they do for a living. So "here's to you" from the guy with the notebook and the kids who showed up at the front gates of dozens of New York cemeteries and said, "Excuse me, but could you please help me find the grave of …"

I would also like to give a heartfelt thanks to the management and staff of two excellent statewide magazines who carried my articles for so many years. Both *Kaatskill Life* and *New York Alive* did great jobs of showcasing my research for a number of years.

In my own hometown of Oneonta, New York, I would like to pay tribute to the *excellent* libraries available for all to use. Hartwick College and SUNY Oneonta were places you could usually find me, crouched over old papers, books, or microfilms in my early days of research. They are excellent facilities, as is Huntington Memorial Library, Oneonta's community public library. It too is a first-class operation.

To my friend Steve Wade, an inveterate road warrior, a five-decades-long friend and a person who loves a cemetery almost as much as I do—well, Wade, you will appreciate this book more than almost anybody I know. Thanks to Doug Decker for putting up with my stories for almost twenty years, and insisting that he still enjoys them. Thanks to Cameron Oliver for a superb job making the book come to life on the Internet at www.NewYorkGraves.com. And to Brian Levis, your help on the photographs was invaluable.

On a personal note, I give thanks to my wonderful family who has offered me support and encouragement for many, many years. To all the D'Imperios in Sidney, New York, and parts far-flung, I say thank you. And thanks to my kids, who made doing this book so much fun. To Frances and Katie, both terrific companions on my treks around the state when they were just little girls, well, here's the book, kids! I would not trade those days of us together in the car for anything. I love you both.

And to the "new" kids on the block, Abby and Joey, thanks for your exuberance and willingness to do it all over again with me ten years later. I never thought I'd have the pleasure of hearing a little one scream, "I found it! I found it!" again. I am glad we will have those memories. Spend your dollar rewards wisely!

And to Trish, well, honey, how lucky was I to marry an English teacher! As you could tell when you read this for the first time … *I needed it*! Thanks for nudging me along and helping me get this thing done. You're the best, and as our favorite gravestone (Robert Frost's) reads, "Wing to Wing; Oar to Oar" forever.

Introduction

The date was Saturday, November 14, 1987, and I had come to bury Kate Smith, "America's First Lady of Song."

I had known Kathryn (as she liked to be called) for many years, having met her in 1967. She was one of our country's most famous and popular entertainers for nearly all of the twentieth century. Much of her fame came by way of "God Bless America," Irving Berlin's love song to his adopted country. Kate Smith had virtually made it our nation's second national anthem. And now, almost a full year after her death, Kathryn was being laid to rest in a large pink mausoleum in her beloved adopted home of Lake Placid, New York. Having summered there for nearly four decades, Kate was a familiar sight at local functions, shopping on Main Street, or zooming along in her speedboat on the lake. Hundreds had joined together at St. Agnes Cemetery to say goodbye to this good lady: fans, friends, neighbors, politicians, and just plain ordinary folks. Her tomb was covered with a large canvas, and just before the services, it was lifted.

Being the only mausoleum at St. Agnes, surely no one would ever be hard pressed to find *this* famous gravesite, I thought. I then noticed something peculiar. The large letters chiseled above her monument read KATHRYN E. SMITH. How many unsuspecting visitors will pass through this beautiful cemetery and never make the connection that this is the final resting place of one of the most famous Americans ever? That this was in fact *the* Kate Smith who had thrilled generations with her unforgettable voice? I tucked that thought away in the back of my mind. Prayers were uttered, hymns were sung, holy water was splashed, and the ceremony came to an end.

We now go back three months prior, to August 17, 1987, and the place is Woodlawn Cemetery in Elmira, New York. I was among less than a dozen people who had come to bury Louis D'Imperio, my grandfather. Grandpa had almost made it to one hundred, having lived to within weeks of the century mark. He had come to America from Italy as a young man, chasing his dreams of a better life. A self-taught musician, but a shoemaker by trade, Grandpa was being buried in Elmira (a town I doubt he had ever visited) because his second wife wanted him there with her family. A diminutive man who enjoyed excellent health for all but six months of his extraordinary life, Grandpa was buried in an extremely large and heavy coffin. Four men (myself included) broke into a sweat just trying to get the coffin from the hearse to the gravesite.

After his burial, my father and I strolled around Woodlawn for a few peaceful moments before our long ride home. As I walked down the path from my grandfather's grave and made a turn near an old elm tree, I was stopped in my tracks by the sight before me. There, larger than life, was the tall, imposing grave monument of one of America's most famous writers, Mark Twain! I studied the marker, took note of the names and dates on the stones around it, and admired the likeness of Twain on the tall obelisk. I found that he too had ended up in Elmira for much the same reason that my grandfather had, because his wife wanted him there! I remember thinking then about what the reactions of my siblings would be when they stumbled upon the grave of the "Ol' Riverboater" as they came to visit Grandpa at Woodlawn. Who would have thought that the immigrant shoemaker and the sage writer would have shared *anything* much less the same final resting place?

On the way home from Kate Smith's funeral, I kept replaying the Lake Placid and Elmira similarities, and wondered aloud if there might be many, or *any*, other interesting graves of famous legends in Upstate New York. A quick mental list, fashioned in just minutes, recalled a visit to FDR's home in Hyde Park, where he is buried, and the school trip I took to nearby Cooperstown, New York, to visit the grave of James Fenimore Cooper. I remembered John Brown, the abolitionist, was buried somewhere in the Adirondack Mountains and that President Chester Arthur's grave was in my college city of Albany. A friend told me later that Grandma Moses was from Upstate New York and was undoubtedly buried there, and that because the American Revolution took place largely in our region I would find some famous graves from that era. So was my list cobbled together, randomly at first and off the top of my head.

Then I started keeping a list, reading research books in my public library, and scouring old newspapers for obituaries (always looking especially for the "and he/she is buried at ..." paragraph). Biographies were helpful (going right to the final chapter, of course). Soon my list became a dozen then two dozen and soon more than fifty! Hence *Great Graves of Upstate New York*.

Keeping my eyes and ears open for "new finds," I soon was hooked on the idea of writing a book about the Upstate New York graves of famous legends. Early on I decided that my border for considering where Upstate started would be the Tappan Zee Bridge across the Hudson River. There are burial reference books regarding New York City graves, but none concerning just those in the large Upstate region. Upstate New York is certainly rich in history and is also filled with enormous natural beauty. It is populated with famous small towns (like Cooperstown and Woodstock) and mid-size cities (like Utica and Syracuse). There is *much* history in this region, and I found it to be a treasure trove of famous burial sites.

I started keeping a more comprehensive list and checked and rechecked my facts. I ultimately realized that if *Great Graves* was to be a definitive work of research and facts I would have to visit each and every grave that I wrote about. That was the start of a wonderful decade-long journey around the state, covering some five thousand miles and two hundred cemeteries in total … and all in beautiful Upstate New York! From the Hudson Valley to the Niagara Frontier and from the Canadian border to the Catskill Mountains, there is hardly a back road I haven't driven on or rural cemetery that I haven't visited.

Some people are shocked when they hear of my "hobby." They think of a cemetery as a sad, almost ghoulish place. Not me. I think of a cemetery as a tangible bridge to the past. As a journal of a certain place or region. There is nothing I like better, particularly on a gorgeous autumn day, than to wander a quaint rural cemetery in New York. The stones tell of this unnamed place, wherever it might be. You can figure out who were the founders, who had money and who didn't, and who fought in what war. Much can be told from deciphering these silent sentinels to the past.

I came up with much data from my cemetery visits. I did have some dead ends (pun intended). Several famous people were cremated and therefore no grave is ever found (Leon Czolgosz, the assassin of President William McKinley, for example; and journalist Edward R. Murrow). Others, after much research, were discovered to be buried just *over* the New York State line, preventing them from being included in this book (Robert Frost is buried in Bennington, Vermont, just a few miles from the New York State border, and you can *almost* see Zane Grey's grave from the banks of the Delaware River in Barryville when peering over into Lackawaxen, Pennsylvania, but, alas I can't include either of them in this book [hey, I just did!]). Still others just simply were impossible to locate (Lester Howe, for example, the discoverer of Howe's Caverns outside of Cobleskill, rests eternally in a grave even the Cavern employees couldn't direct me to).

Despite all this, my journey was exciting and informative, and grave or no grave, I wouldn't have missed a mile of it. And what a way to see New York State! I have sloshed through the snowy back roads of the Finger Lakes region in December, and careened around S-turns high in the Adirondacks in the fall. For the sake of reference, the southernmost grave in this book is Admiral John Worden, captain of the famous Civil War ironclad *The Monitor*, in Pawling; the northernmost grave belongs to singer Kate Smith in Lake Placid; the westernmost grave is that of Lucille Ball in Jamestown; and the easternmost is the grave of poet Edna St. Vincent Millay in Austerlitz.

Most of the seventy legends in *Great Graves* have easily recognizable names. Goodrich means tires. Serling means *The Twilight Zone*. Emily Post means manners. Cornell and Vassar mean education. Grossinger means hotel. So it was of even more interest to me when I could find the Upstate graves of unsung legends whose stories I found most fascinating and, for the most part, untold. In this book, you will find the stories of Mr. Wells and Mr. Fargo, the *real* Maid of the Mist, the author of The Pledge of Allegiance, the "Shoemaker to the World," "The Yankee Leaper," "The Priest of the Poor," "The Sage of Slabsides," and even "Old Bones." They are all buried in Upstate New York.

It is the intention of *Great Graves* to be a multipurpose book. First and foremost, it is a definitive research guide to the final resting places of the included legends. I have personally visited all graves, and explicit directions to them have been included. Photographs of many of the graves are included as well.

Secondly, it is a biographical "sketchbook" of all seventy entries. This is *not* a scholarly, encyclopedic dissertation on their lives and deeds, for that was never the intention (it is all about the *graves* remember). Still there are many tidbits I felt I should pass on to the curious reader. Each of these bits fills out the profiles of the different entries. For example, I had no intention of combing through the more than twelve years of the FDR administration and repeating all of the data within. I'll leave that to the historians. But did you know FDR is buried with his pets? I had no intention of cataloging singer Kate Smith's three thousand recordings, but I found it interesting that this lady who entertained millions with her voice could not speak a word until she was four years old! The great naturalist John Burroughs has been the subject of dozens of books, yet I found it most interesting that when he knew it was his time to die, he boarded a train in California and said (basically), "Take me back to Upstate New York." (He died en route.) Or that Dr. Mary Walker, the *only* female to ever win the Congressional Medal of Honor was buried *wearing it!* Or that Ernie Davis, the first black Heisman Trophy winner, had his football jersey retired *before* he ever played a complete professional football game. Or that one of the richest men in America, Russell Sage, was so worried about grave robbers that he had a burglar alarm installed in his tomb! Or that George F. Johnson's funeral was the largest funeral ever held for a private citizen at the time of his death! These are some of the unusual, bizarre (and admit it, *fun*) facts that I wanted to share with my readers.

And thirdly, *Great Graves,* to a large extent, is a unique travelogue to the far reaches of the Empire State. Each entry contains information about museums, historic sites, tours, landmarks, Websites, and other pertinent information to make your trip down the footpaths of history more enjoyable.

Part reference, part factoid, part fun, and part travel. It has been an interesting journey for me over the years, and I hope *Great Graves of Upstate New York* is a book you will stuff under the front seat of your car and pull out whenever you get the itch to take "the road less traveled" and pay a visit to some of the most colorful and important residents of our great state.

—Chuck D'Imperio
Oneonta, New York
www.NewYorkGraves.com

Contents

GEORGE CLINTON_____

"The Father of New York"

In the pantheon of legendary New Yorkers, surely no name would shine brighter than that of its first governor, George Clinton. An astute politician of untiring ambition, he was one of the most popular leaders of his (or any other) time. From his early political beginnings in his home area, Ulster County, George Clinton would rise to lead his state for an unprecedented *seven terms* as governor and then go on to become vice president under both Jefferson and Madison!

A lifelong resident of New York's Catskill Country, he was called on to lead the defenses of the Hudson River Valley during the hostilities of 1775. His military career was described as lackluster, and he oversaw the defeat of his forces at the hands of the British on more than one occasion (including the surrender of Fort Montgomery and the burning of Esopus in 1777). Clinton never pretended to possess great military skills and was eager to move into his more natural arena of politics. A regrettable footnote to his undistinguished military career is the fact that his soldierly duties prevented him from

1

attending the signing of the Declaration of Independence, thereby missing the glorious opportunity to affix his signature to the most famous document in American history!

Once well-pointed along his political journey, George Clinton proved to be unstoppable. In June of 1777, he defeated the well-known Philip Schuyler in the gubernatorial race by such a lopsided margin that he was elected to *both* the governorship and the lieutenant-governorship (he resigned from the latter post). He earned a sterling reputation as a tight-fisted financial manager and as an adroit negotiator.

An iron-horse in New York politics, Clinton served as governor for an astounding twenty-one years! Some of his elections were squeakers, more were lopsided victories. As a fighter for New York's future, he supported greater manufacturing growth, better schools and roads, and greater power for the states in the realm of internal affairs (he was a vocal anti-federalist). His interest in establishing a sophisticated interconnecting series of waterways and canals to join the Hudson River with the Great Lakes was championed later by his famous nephew, DeWitt Clinton, who also became a New York governor.

George Clinton was born on July 26, 1739, and died on April 20, 1812. He never retired from public life and was the sitting vice president of the United States at the time of his death.

Buried originally in the Congressional Cemetery in Washington, D.C., his body was moved to Kingston, New York, in 1908, where it was ceremoniously re-interred in the historic cemetery at the Old Dutch Church. The cemetery is located in the old downtown section of Kingston, next to Ulster Savings Bank. His tall monument can be viewed from the sidewalk and is marked by a commemorative plaque. His gravesite was the source of great historical interest in 1989, the marking of the 250th anniversary of his birth. At that time, his imposing gravestone was cleaned and restored to its original grandeur.

As we begin our look at the Upstate New York gravesites of seventy American legends in this book, a trip down the footpaths of history would be well-started with a reflective visit to this quiet, tree-shaded spot that holds the remains of a true son of the Hudson Valley, Governor George Clinton, "The Father of New York."

Author's note: A most interesting side trip while visiting the grave of Governor Clinton is to enter and inspect the beautiful Old Reformed Protestant Dutch Church, in whose cemetery he is buried. It is a gorgeous place of worship and is one of the oldest churches in the Hudson Valley. Throughout Kingston, once the capital of New York (the British torched the city in 1777), you will find many historic locations. The Old Reformed Protestant Dutch Church is one of the most beautiful buildings in the downtown area and is open for viewing during standard business hours (845-338-6759). The church was formed in 1659. The church and historic graveyard are located at 272 Wall Street, in downtown ("Old Town") Kingston.

ANNIE EDSON TAYLOR

"Niagara's Maid of the Mist"

Tour boats chugging through the whitewaters of the Niagara Falls basin bear the name of the mythical "Maid of the Mist." But make no *myth*take about it … Annie Edson Taylor was the *real* "Maid of the Mist," the first person to ever go over mighty Niagara in a barrel and live to tell about it!

On October 24, 1901, the sixty-something widowed schoolteacher entered a rickety, old, pickle barrel and launched herself over the 158-foot Horseshoe Falls at Niagara in a desperate attempt to grasp fame's brass ring. *And she did it!* Strapped into place inside the homemade vessel by leather strips to keep her immobile, a bicycle pump for air tucked under her arm, and a one-hundred-pound blacksmith's anvil between her legs to keep her upright, Taylor plunged into the whirlpool below the falls and disappeared for a heart-stopping seventeen minutes. The crowd that had gathered went silent as they waited for either her barrel to pop up from the foam or for her lifeless body to wash up on the rocks.

A cheer went up when the battered pickle barrel with the words "Queen of the Mist" hand-painted on the side shot up out of the water and drifted to the shore. Friends wrestled the barrel to land and smashed it open with a sledgehammer. Inside they found tiny Annie Taylor unconscious and bleeding from a head gash, but very much alive! In a few moments, she came to and, still wearing her best dress and high heels, strode ashore to the applause of the wide-eyed throng. News cameras captured the moment she reached land. Her first public comment was, "Nobody ought ever do that again!"

Headlines screamed her miraculous ride over Niagara on the front pages of newspapers around the world. In a rush to cash in on her publicity stunt (making money was the reason she did it in the first place), she appeared to great exclamation nine days later at the nearby Pan American Exposition on its closing day. Declared the "highlight of the entire show," Taylor sat regally in a high-backed chair, still a bit unsteady from her stunt, and with nary a word or handshake, simply acknowledged the more than three thousand onlookers as they streamed by her in awe. With no business manager or public relations guidance, she began a busy nationwide tour that was ill-conceived and poorly scheduled. She spoke in front of large crowds for little or no pay, wrote a ten-page booklet titled *Over The Falls*, which failed to sell, and spent any income she made foolishly and with abandon. Within the year, other jumpers and daredevils took her place in the public spotlight and interest in her waned. She was soon broke and obscure.

When Annie Edson Taylor died on April 10, 1921, she was blind and a pauper in the Welfare Ward of the Niagara County Home. She is buried in Oakwood Cemetery, where the echo of the Horseshoe Falls can still be heard.

Author's note: Taylor is buried in "Heroes Corner," also known as the "Strangers Rest" section of Oakwood Cemetery, at 763 Portage Road, Niagara Falls, New York. For cemetery information, call 716-284-5131. Her gravestone reads, "ANNIE EDSON TAYLOR: FIRST TO GO OVER HORSESHOE FALLS IN A BARREL AND LIVE, OCT. 24, 1901." Interestingly, no birth date is noted. Although unsure about her exact age at the time of her ride over the falls, many believe that she was in her sixties at the time of her death.

Enter Oakwood and veer to the right. Continue through to Section 8. She is buried three rows into this section. This "Heroes Corner" includes the graves of many other jumpers, barrel-riders, and daredevils who challenged Niagara over the years. Taylor is buried next to Carlisle Graham, whose tombstone remembers that he was "the first to go through the Whirlpool Rapids of Niagara on July 11, 1886." His stone is identical to Annie's. Another interesting gravesite belongs to Captain Matthew Webb, the first man to ever swim the English Channel. He swam the channel on August 24,

1875, dressed in a handmade red satin swimming costume. On July 21, 1883, he tried to swim *under* Niagara Falls. He entered the basin below the falls and quickly got sucked into the whirlpool and drowned. He was wearing the same red satin costume from his Channel swim. He is buried near Annie's grave. A replica of Taylor and her barrel are among the most popular scenes at the Ripley's Believe It Or Not Museum on the Canadian side of the falls.

ROD SERLING

"The Gatekeeper to the Twilight Zone"

A recent entertainment magazine honored the "Immortals of Television," naming twelve of the guiding lights and brightest stars of early TV. The impact left by these show-business giants is undeniable ... Lucille Ball, Milton Berle, Jackie Gleason, Walter Cronkite, Ed Sullivan, and others. Each name brings to mind a vivid trademark, a definitive characteristic that instantly conjures up the golden years of TV—Lucy stuffing her mouth with chocolates while trying to keep up with an assembly line gone berserk; "Uncle Miltie" raising cross-dressing to a fine art; Gleason's Ralph Kramden bellowing, "One of these days, Alice, BAM! ... to the moon!"; Cronkite's "And that's the way it is"; and Sullivan's "Really big shew." It is then quite interesting to note that among these three-dimensional, larger-than-life characters, another immortal is recognized as one of the icons of early television. He was not outrageous or bombastic, nor was he a clown or even an actor. He was a quiet, shy, unassuming writer who created a show that remains, decades after it first aired, one of the most popular and critically acclaimed programs of all time. His name was Rod Serling, and his show was *The Twilight Zone*.

Rod Serling's magical gift to television was an ingenious, macabre imagination, which he translated so brilliantly to the American public through his scripts and teleplays. So vivid were the fruits of his imagination that, even after all of these years, *The Twilight Zone* episodes remain as fresh and as clear in our minds as they were the first time we saw them.

After going to school in the Binghamton, New York, area as a youth, Serling attended Antioch College, where he wrote and sold his first television script. It didn't take long for his unique talents to be recognized by the studios in New York and California, and soon he found steady employment as a scriptwriter. He was honored early on for one of his first pieces, *Patterns* (1955), a searing look at boardroom-level desperation in corporate America (timely?). In the 1960s, he wrote several classic movie scripts, including *Requiem for a Heavyweight* (1963), *Seven Days in May* (1964), *Assault on a Queen* (1966), and *Planet of the Apes* (1967). All were warmly received by both critics and audiences.

Despite his success in the movie industry, there can be no doubt that Rod Serling's real memorial is the television series *The Twilight Zone* (and later *Night Gallery*). Each episode took the viewer down a twisting path of incredible tension, subtle humor, bizarre visual effects, and wildly flip-flopping endings. Shot in the black-and-white of its era, *The Twilight Zone* still mesmerizes audiences with its on-the-edge storylines and haunting messages.

Serling liked to use movie stars from Hollywood's past as featured performers in his episodes of the two programs. It is in these particular shows that he produced some of his most memorable vignettes. Who can ever forget Ed Wynn as the desperate timekeeper trying to "keep time" with his timepieces? Or blind Joan Crawford regaining her sight during a power blackout? Or Burgess Meredith as the timid banker who is finally alone with his beloved books but possesses no glasses with which to read them? Most vivid of all was "The Invaders," an episode of *The Twilight Zone* that aired on January 21, 1961. In it, screen legend Agnes Moorehead played a lonely old crone whose ramshackle house is invaded by tiny space aliens. With virtually no dialogue, a frenetic pace of action, stark sets and lighting, and the intense acting technique of Ms. Moorehead, this tale of defending one's home from unseen outsiders made for one of the most harrowing and unforgettable nights of the year.

Rod Serling was born on Christmas Day in 1924 and died June 28, 1975, following heart surgery. He is buried in beautiful Lakeview Cemetery in Interlaken, New York, in the Finger Lakes region of the state (take Route 96 north out of Ithaca). It is interesting to note that this man, who has been called one of television's immortals, is buried beneath a simple government-issued veteran's marker that makes no mention of his contribution to the world of entertainment. Instead, it modestly reads, "Rodman E. Serling TEC5 US Army World War II."

Author's note: It is difficult, but not impossible, to find Serling's grave. The cemetery has no markings to lead you there, but you will find his gravesite on the eastern end of the cemetery, nearest Cayuga Lake, six rows in from the boundary of the property (Section Two, O). The village of Interlaken is a quaint community in the heart of New York's wine region. Rod Serling's hometown, Binghamton, New York, remembers him with a star on the city's "Walk of Fame," a film festival, and other memorials. His actual home, at 67 Bennett Avenue, was featured in the *X-Files* television program as a homage, and the address was also used by Serling himself in "They're Tearing Down Tim Riley's Bar," an Emmy Award-nominated episode of *Night Gallery*.

GEORGE F. JOHNSON

"Shoemaker to the World"

"As long as children are born barefoot, E-J will sell shoes!"

George F. Johnson, co-founder and head of the Endicott-Johnson Shoe Company ("E-J"), was a man of the people, a sage thinker, and a compassionate innovator. He led E-J from its start as a smokestack factory in Binghamton, New York, to "E-J, The Concept." He developed Upstate New York's rural Southern Tier into his own little petri dish of "welfare capitalism" and earned a degree of unabashed adoration from his workers that is still felt along the banks of the Susquehanna River more than a half-century after his death. Oh, and along the way, he turned Endicott-Johnson Shoe Co. into the world's second largest maker of footwear!

When "George F," as he was called, arrived in rural Binghamton in 1881 to join Henry Endicott as part owner of the Lester Brothers Boot Company, his vision of where he wanted to take his labor philosophies was unbridled. Although he arrived with nothing ("13-

cents in my pocket and minus a collar," he said), he was a man rich with ideas. When partner Endicott died in 1920 and Johnson became the sole owner of E-J, his long-planned policy of a "Square Deal" for his workers was fully implemented. As a testament to his success, even today a grand Romanesque archway adorns the Main Street entrance to Johnson City, New York, proclaiming, "Welcome to the Home of the Square Deal."

In his quest to turn the Southern Tier into a "Valley of Opportunity," E-J's 18,000 workers benefited greatly from George F's industrial democracy, and they would never forget him for it. There were E-J playgrounds for the children, E-J homes for the workers (provided at below market prices), E-J health care policies, and even one of the nation's first revenue sharing plans. He offered the highest working wage in the industry and the best working conditions of any factory anywhere. He instituted one of the first eight-hour workdays in America and provided steady employment through thick and thin. In fact, in the more than four decades that George F ran his company, it never suffered a shutdown or a strike. Legend has it that when George F was faced with terrible economic times during the Great Depression, he still managed to keep over half his employees working, and for the benefit of those he did have to lay off, he opened up his own private dining hall and handed out free meals.

Perhaps the most anticipated and appreciated "benefit" of all was the "E-J Annual Picnic." These parties resembled a cross between a county fair and a revival meeting, and they are *still* talked about by older citizens of the Triple Cities. One "E-J May Day Celebration" counted nearly 25,000 attendees.

Was this all merely forward-looking liberalism? Was this a sincere attempt on the part of management to ease the burden of the working class? Or was this simply a veiled variation of the old "carrot and stick" way of doing business? Some of that era thought old George F had set up a twentieth-century feudal system where the "grateful serfs" (the factory workers) owe eternally to the benevolent king (Johnson) and toil tirelessly for the kingdom (E-J). Whatever side you may agree with, there is no disagreement with the fact that George F. Johnson was a much-loved man.

"The First Citizen of the Triple Cities" (Binghamton, Endicott, and the one which is named after him, Johnson City, New York) was born on October 14, 1857, and died at the age of ninety-one on November 28, 1948. His body lay in state in the parlor of his private residence on Park Street, just across from the main entrance to his factory. More than 10,000 mourners passed through his home to pay their respects, many dressed in workers' clothes and weeping uncontrollably in front of the open casket. Later his funeral was held at En-Joie Park, which he had built. At the park, his body was again made available for viewing and another 50,000 passed by. All schools, industries, and retail stores were shuttered at 12:30 PM on the day of the funeral as thousands stayed home to listen to the service on the radio (all four of the area radio stations covered the event live). One national reporter called it "the single largest funeral ceremony for a private citizen ever held in the United States."

To reach the grave of the "Shoemaker to the World," travel west on NYS Route 17 through the Binghamton, New York, area, exiting at Endwell. Follow the signs for 17-C west along the feeder road about two miles. This becomes East Main Street, Endicott, New York. Riverhurst Cemetery comes up quickly on your left. As you turn into the main gate of Riverhurst, you will see a mausoleum straight ahead reading JOHNSON. This is the family plot. Stroll around behind it, and you will see the massive headstone bearing the signature of Johnson scrawled across its face, signifying his final resting place.

Author's note: Johnson's "Valley of Opportunity" has fallen on hard times recently. In the decade of the 1980s, the leading industry in the Southern Tier, IBM, drastically began cutting its workforce. Thousands were laid off and moved out of the valley. It is hard to imagine how George F would have dealt with the economic crunch that impacted his hometown so severely. In any case, Endicott-Johnson, facing stiff competition from European shoe manufacturers, has vanished as a local shoe manufacturer. The last small E-J clerical office closed in 2005, ending a storied decades-long relationship between the company and the community. Where thousands of immigrants poured into the Southern Tier in the beginning of the twentieth century, speaking only one phrase in English ("Which way E-J?"), now only hulking remains of enormous workshops are left. During World War II, Endicott-Johnson made more than 25 million pairs of shoes for the military *alone*. In 2005, the last E-J building closed and the company vanished from George F's beloved "Home of the Square Deal."

Harriet Tubman

"A Woman Called Moses"

For most of us, the whole concept of slavery seems so immoral and indecent that we find it hard to believe that it occurred in our country at all. But it did happen, and it became the benchmark of a turning point in American history, standing out as the most controversial issue during a time of great fear and divisiveness in our nation. Out of those terrible times came the courageous figures that we all learned about in high school, figures entrusted with the care and safety of frightened slaves fleeing the shackles of bondage in the South to a new beginning in the North. They were known as "conductors," and they journeyed on the fabled route to freedom called the "Underground Railroad." None was more heroic, more colorful, or more inspiring than Harriet Tubman.

Tubman was a daring and fearless "escort" to hundreds of escaping slaves and won the respect of men and women alike (and friend and foe alike!) for her cunning and inventiveness in completing her flights of freedom. She ultimately made nineteen trips along the imaginary railroad route to freedom, guiding more than three hundred slaves to safety.

The Compromise Act of 1850 segmented the nation into free and slave states. A provision of the act required citizens to aid in the arrest and return of fugitive slaves who were trying to reach the North. This provision accelerated the abolitionist movement and gave rise to the Underground Railroad, especially during the period of 1850 to 1860. The act preserved the unity of the nation in the short run, but sowed the seeds of racism and brought upon the Civil War.

At one time Harriet Tubman had a $40,000 bounty on her head (dead or alive) and was sought by whole armies of men. She bragged that she never failed to complete a successful mission. Coldly unafraid, she would often threaten the nervous or fainthearted fugitives with a loaded pistol, ensuring the completion of their escape to the North.

Harriet Tubman's courage and passion were an inspiration to people of all walks of life. She served her country unselfishly for decades, both as a conductor and as a nurse and Union scout during the war. Her autumnal years were spent in Upstate New York, where she received visitors regularly and never tired of retelling the thrilling stories of her days as one of the most vocal and important opponents of slavery in America. When she died at age ninety-two, on March 10, 1913, she was mourned nationally as "an American treasure."

Harriet Tubman rests eternally at Fort Hill Cemetery, 19 Fort Street in Auburn, New York. Hers is the most famous of many famous names buried here, and the front office will gladly give you precise instructions to the whereabouts of her gravesite (under a towering Norwegian spruce tree in the West Lawn section). Her tombstone reads, "To The Memory Of Harriet Tubman Davis. Heroine Of The Underground Railroad. Nurse And Scout In The Civil War. Servant Of God. WELL DONE!" (Davis was her second husband.)

Author's note: Fort Hill Cemetery (315-253-8132) lists many famous "residents," including Jerome Holland, the first African American to head the New York Stock Exchange; Theodore Case, who created the first movie soundtrack; Myles Keogh, a soldier killed at Little Big Horn; and Louis Lawton, a Congressional Medal of Honor winner. Tubman's home is now a much-visited landmark at 180 South Street in Auburn (315-252-2081; E-mail at hthome@localnet. com). Harriet Tubman had many friends in high places. None was closer to her, or more powerful, than her friend William H. Seward, Secretary of War under Abraham Lincoln and also U.S. Senator from New York. The engineer of "Seward's Folly" (the acquisition of Alaska by the United States), Seward gave Tubman the twenty-six acres of land on which she built her home and later a residence for the aged. He was her greatest admirer and a great supporter of her causes, both emotionally and financially. The Harriet Tubman Home is open Tuesday through Friday and Saturdays by appointment only. Ironically, William Seward is buried in Fort Hill Cemetery not far from his friend!

FRANCIS BELLAMY

"I Pledge Allegiance ..."

The New York State historical marker near the cemetery entrance tells of its most famous occupant: "The Grave of Francis Bellamy. Author of The Pledge of Allegiance." Rome Cemetery, in Rome, New York, has seen its fair share of famous names since its incorporation in 1851, but none has brought more notoriety than Francis Bellamy.

The son of a pastor, he was a writer for a magazine called *The Youth's Companion* when, in 1892, he was asked by his editor to write a salute promoting the 400th anniversary Columbus Day. The tribute was to be used by students attending our nation's public schools. Understanding this to mean a "Salute to America," Bellamy came up with the most familiar twenty-three words in American history, words that have been recited for over a century by schoolchildren and adults alike. "I pledge allegiance to my flag and to the republic for which it stands; one nation indivisible, with liberty and justice for all." Minor changes were made through the years. The phrase "under God" was suggested by President Eisenhower in the 1950s.

Bellamy (1855-1931) is buried in the most prominent plot in the Rome Cemetery (Section D, to the right of the entrance), and a plaque bearing testimony to his fame is affixed to his monument. A towering flagpole at this site will guide you to his grave. The words to the Pledge of Allegiance are carved into his gravestone. Rome is located off the New York State Thruway, northwest of Utica. The cemetery is located on Jervis Avenue at Golden Avenue. You will know you are near when you see the old Rome Free Academy School on Turin Street. You are one mile from the cemetery at this point.

Author's note: How timely the entry of Francis Bellamy is to this book. Even he could not imagine the controversy that would surround his "enhanced" pledge 110 years after it was written. The firestorm of criticism over a 2002 high court decision calling the inserted "under God" in the pledge unconstitutional would once again have newspaper writers all over the country scrambling to discover Bellamy and the origin of this once-innocuous paean to America. As recently as the year 2005, courts of varying degrees were questioning the constitutionality of the pledge. Some believed that Bellamy espoused socialistic principles, and one, Rex Curry, has even established a Website (www.rexcurry.net) urging the changing of the names of all schools dedicated to the memory of Francis Bellamy. It has yet to take hold. At 7118 Bennan Avenue, in Rome, stands the campus of Francis Bellamy Elementary School.

GLENN CURTISS

"Pilot's License #1"

Aside from perhaps the Wright brothers, probably no other American contributed more to the development of aviation in America than Glenn H. Curtiss of Hammondsport, New York.

Curtiss's career paralleled that of the Wright brothers, and their paths would cross many times (sometimes with unhappy results). Like Orville and Wilbur, Curtiss began by building motorcycle engines. In 1907, he raced his cycle at speeds over 136 miles per hour, an astonishing speed at the time, and was dubbed by the international press as "The Fastest Man on Earth."

Here in tiny Hammondsport, now a sleepy little Finger Lakes community in Upstate New York, but then the hub of all American aviation activity, Curtiss flew the first witnessed flight of one kilometer in the country on the Fourth of July, 1908.

Curtiss was a most energetic advocate of the use of aviation in the military. During World War I, his Curtiss Aeroplane Company was the largest manufacturer of aircraft in the nation. In 1919, a

Navy-Curtiss "flying boat," commanded by Albert C. Reid, made the very first flight across the Atlantic Ocean. Curtiss chalked up several other historic firsts, including becoming the first naval instructor of air pilots. In 1910, he won $10,000 in cash in a contest sponsored by *The New York World* newspaper, which was looking for the fastest flight time from Albany, New York, to New York City. Curtiss did it in an amazing two hours and fifty-one minutes!

In one of the most famous meetings of Curtiss and the Wright brothers, the result was a long-lasting feud between these pioneering legends. In 1908, Curtiss had built his first airplane, "The June Bug." It was controlled by a new innovation called ailerons (wing flaps). Perhaps with their noses more than slightly out of joint, the Wright brothers filed a patent infringement suit against Curtiss for using what they claimed was their flight control mechanism. The court ruled in favor of the Wright brothers. On October 13, 1924, Curtiss was featured on the cover of *TIME* magazine.

In his later years, he and his partner, James Bright, were the largest land speculators in southeastern Florida, where they intended to establish a premier flying school. Curtiss eventually became the founder of what are today three vibrant Florida cities: Hialeah, Miami Springs, and Opa-Locka.

Glenn Curtiss was born on May 21, 1878, and died at the age of only fifty-two while undergoing surgery in a Buffalo hospital (July 23, 1930). He is buried in his beloved hometown. In all the years of accolades and honors, Curtiss always said that he was proudest of one thing: his pilot's license. He was officially issued "U.S. Pilot's License Number One" as a tribute to his soaring achievements. (It is interesting to note that Curtiss's fame was so widespread that France awarded him its own national Pilot's License Number Two!)

Hammondsport, New York, is situated among the gently rolling hills of New York's beautiful Finger Lakes region, on the southern tip of Keuka Lake. A sign welcomes the visitor to the community declaring "Hammondsport, The Cradle of Aviation." Pleasant

Valley Cemetery is located one mile north of town on Route 34. You will have no difficulty finding the huge, craggy boulder, inscribed "CURTISS," marking his final resting place.

Author's note: Hammondsport is extremely proud of its famous native son and hosts a very interesting museum dedicated to his life and the early history of American aviation. The Curtiss Museum is located at 8419 Route 54. There is a small admission charge, and it is open year round. Many changing exhibits and interactive displays make this a popular tourist attraction for the aviation buff and others (www.linkny.com/curtissmuseum). Phone 607-569-2160 for more information about this shrine to "The Henry Ford of Aviation."

LUCILLE BALL

"We All Loved Lucy"

Lucille Ball was the undisputed "Queen of Comedy." She was born in and raised around Celeron, New York, just outside Jamestown. She lived more than fifty years in Hollywood, where she became an iconic figure of the entertainment scene. Lucy died in 1989 and was buried in Forest Lawn ("The Cemetery of the Stars") in Los Angeles. The call to come home was just too great, however, and she was re-interred in Lake View Cemetery in Jamestown in 2003. Today she is buried with her beloved mother (Desiree, who died in 1977 at age eighty-five) and her dad (Henry, who died of typhoid fever in 1915 at only twenty-eight when Lucy was four). Below her name on the family grave marker it simply says, "You've Come Home."

It is pointless to try to list every great "Lucy moment," for really, we all know each and every one of them—the stomping on the grapes in the Italian barrel, dressing as Superman with actor George Reeves, trying to keep up with the maniacal candy conveyor belt, getting drunk while filming a vitamin commercial, and on and on and on. But there are some interesting Lucy-factoids you might not know.

Lucille Ball made more than 110 films, from *The Bowery* (1933) to her acclaimed performance as a street-smart street woman in CBS television's *Stone Pillow* (1985 at age seventy-four). Appropriately, one of her Hollywood Walk of Fame stars is for her movie work (it is located at 6436 Hollywood Boulevard). On television she was America's most popular star for decades. From the classic *I Love Lucy* (first aired in 1951) to *The Lucy-Desi Comedy Hour* (1957) to *The Lucy Show* (1962) to *Here's Lucy!* (1968) and to *Life with Lucy* (1986), she was a constant friend and "neighbor" to millions over several generations. Also appropriately, one of her Hollywood Walk of Fame stars is for her television career (it is located at 6104 Hollywood Boulevard).

Lucy won every major show-business award ever created. She won four Emmy Awards (1953, 1956, 1967, and 1968) for her shows. She was an early inductee into the Comedy Hall of Fame and the Television Hall of Fame. She received the highest arts award, The Kennedy Center Honors, in 1986. She was inducted into the National Women's Hall of Fame in 2002. Lucy (and baby Desi, Jr.) graced the very first edition of *TV Guide*, and she would eventually rack up a record thirty-one cover appearances. On her birthday in 2001, she was honored with her own U.S. postage stamp.

Lucy was famous for inviting all of her celebrity friends to appear on her popular TV shows, and they all looked forward to doing so. Among the most frequent guests were Milton Berle and Tennessee Ernie Ford (five appearances each), Ann Southern and Jack Benny (six appearances each), and others. Carol Burnett, perhaps Lucy's closest celebrity "girl-friend," appeared a record seven times on the various Lucy shows and also joined her for a well-received 1967 television special. Lucy's Kennedy Center award was followed by Carol getting her own in 2003. It is eerie to note that Lucy died on April 26, Carol Burnett's birthday. (Lucy fans will no doubt note that character actress Mary Jane Croft, who remained extremely close to Lucy both professionally and privately until the TV star's death, appeared many, many times on all of the Lucy programs.)

Lucille Ball was the first woman to own her own studio (Desilu) and wielded great power in the early days of television. She married Cuban bandleader Desi Arnaz and had two children (Lucie, born in 1951 before *I Love Lucy*; and Desi, Jr., who was born in 1953 with a record 44 million viewers following his mom's pregnancy right up to his arrival). Lucy and Desi split in 1960, and she married stand-up comic Gary Morton in 1961. He survived her.

Apparently Lucy was a little bit suspicious about the letters A and R. Her television characters were Lucy Ri*c*a*r*do, Lucy C*ar*michael, Lucy C*ar*ter, and finally Lucy B*ar*ker.

In gradually declining health, Lucy made two appearances on her favorite game show in her final years. She appeared on special celebrity editions of *Password* in 1987 and 1988. She was an aggressive and inveterate game-player, and in fact, the Milton Bradley Company, a leader in home games, convinced Lucy to sponsor her own board game called *Body Language*, a pantomime contest. Of course, her prowess at backgammon was legendary among her friends.

Lucille Ball made her final appearance before a camera on March 29, 1989, when she and Bob Hope presented the Best Picture Oscar at the 62nd Academy Awards Show. The quintessential Hollywood cigarette smoker, she would be dead just four weeks later of a ruptured aorta.

Lucy is buried in Lake View Cemetery, Jamestown, New York.

Author's note: Probably more has been written about the life and career of Lucille Ball than any other star. The whole of Jamestown has embraced the Lucy mystique unabashedly. Visitors wander the center-city area seeking out the towering murals on the side of city buildings depicting great Lucy moments (the scene of her and Ethel at the candy conveyor belt, etc.). Even the front of the main post office is adorned with a giant replica of the Lucy-Desi postage stamp. Many stores carry tributes to Lucy in their windows, displays of varying tastes. The main lobby of the downtown Holiday Inn (and ground zero for Lucy fans during the festivals) features a giant watercolor of Lucille Ball relaxing in a beautiful blue gown. The sign explains, "This painting hung in Lucy's Beverly Hills home for many years." A definitive repository for "everything Lucy" is the popular Lucy-Desi Museum in Jamestown. This facility is an affectionate "kiss" to their homegrown star and thousands visit this fun venue every year, whether to attend either of the two weeklong Lucy Festivals (spring and summer) or just to spend a few moments watching some of the old black-and-white shows. The museum is located at 716 Pine Street in downtown Jamestown (far western New York State; www. lucy-desi.com). Lucy now rests eternally with her parents in Lake View Cemetery, Jamestown. Dozens of fans stop by her grave for a poignant visit every day. Enter the first gate to the sixty-eight-acre cemetery and follow the arrows to her grave in the Highland Section (her grave is about one hundred yards from the grave of tire producer B.F. Goodrich, also in this book). Beautiful plantings adorn her gravesite, and personal tributes from fans can be seen nearby. Her gravestone lists family statistics on one side and an "I Love Lucy-style" logo on the back. Her name is listed as Lucille Desiree Ball Morton. There is no mention of Arnaz.

A bizarre footnote to the final resting places of the stars of the old Lucy shows is that there are none! Well, almost none. Husband and co-star Desi Arnaz (d. 1986), Vivian Vance (Ethel Mertz, d. 1979), Gale Gordon (Mr. Mooney, d. 1999), husband Gary Morton (d. 1999), and co-star and close friend Mary Jane Croft (d. 1999) were all cremated with no record existing as to where their ashes are. Only William Frawley (Fred Mertz, d. 1966) was buried in the ground, and he can be found at San Fernando Mission Cemetery, Mission Hills, California.

TIM MURPHY

"The Savior of Schoharie"

Tim Murphy could neither read nor write. He was a simple man with simple tastes. He was rough-hewn and affable, a man of the soil and a lover of nature. He also had the stealth of a ghost and the eye of an eagle. Some say "Ol' Tim" Murphy won the Battle of Saratoga for the Americans single-handedly. Here is his story.

When the British troops were making encroachments against Murphy's home area of Schoharie County, he went into action. The British, fronted by vicious Indian warriors, had been terrorizing the colonists and spreading fear throughout the valley. Murphy, a natural hunter and a man completely at ease in the bosom of nature, began his own little counter-insurgency. In the thick of an area known as Panther Falls, Murphy engaged in a hit-and-run skirmish with an Indian scouting party that lasted for over three days. Through lush forests and over raging mountain streams, Murphy played the Indian game as well as they did. At the end, all *eleven* in the Indian party had been slain by the patient and wily Murphy. Another time, near the same area, Murphy set out to free a white settler, Jennie Swart, who had been kidnapped by four roving Onondaga Indians, including the much-feared Ugly Beaver. He stalked the Indian party for one hundred miles before making his move, killing all the Indians and freeing the young girl.

Murphy's fame grew far and wide as stories of his escapades were told and retold. One time, on a raiding expedition at Canandaigua Lake (in Central New York), Murphy's group was entirely wiped out, save for himself. With pluck and daring, he evaded capture by a force of fifty Seneca Indians. Murphy (an expert marksman) once fired on a British river barge during a battle near Boston, Massachusetts. Even though the boat was a half-mile away, he was able to pick off ten redcoats. His choice of weapon was an unusual double-barreled Golchar rifle with a hand-rubbed oak stock. With it, Murphy said he could "shoot the eye out of a bear at 900 yards out." So feared was his sharpshooting expertise that British General St. Leger, who normally placed an eight-dollar bounty on a Yankee scalp, raised it to sixteen dollars for Murphy's!

On Christmas Day, 1776, Murphy accompanied George Washington across the Delaware River, joined the fabled Dan Morgan's Rifle Corps, and soon became its most valuable member. At the Revolutionary War's greatest battle, Saratoga (or Bemis Heights), Murphy's date with destiny was upon him.

British General Burgoyne attacked American forces with everything he had at Saratoga. The bloodletting was merciless. The British field general, General Simon Fraser, pushed his redcoat army deeper and deeper into American territory. Fraser, resplendent in his flamboyant battle attire, with feathers and plumes flying, sitting high atop a giant white steed, was an intimidating sight. His aide-de-camp, Sir Francis Clark, stayed close to Fraser's side, calculating the enemy losses and planning the army's moves. Dan Morgan, convinced that the American forces were about to meet certain defeat, summoned Tim Murphy to his tent. The task at hand was a simple one, he told Murphy. Both British generals must be killed or the battle would be lost.

Murphy, clutching his trusted Golchar, climbed a tall oak tree near the rim of the battlefield and waited. When the British started approaching the area, Murphy patiently waited for the two of them to enter the same scope view. When Clark was three hundred feet away, Murphy let loose with the first volley. Just seconds later he fired his last shot at Fraser. Both rounds found their deadly mark. With their commanders dead, the British troops scattered and began an open retreat, and the final victory went to the Americans. British General John Burgoyne said later, "If Dan Morgan's riflemen had marched with me, I'd hold Albany by now!"

After the war, Murphy moved back to his Schoharie Valley and lived to the age of sixty-seven. Even today, the story of "Ol' Tim" is taught in the classrooms up and down the valley. Oh, and his story is also kept alive at the Saratoga Battlefield. A marker near the oak tree where Murphy fired off his two decisive shots is highlighted on tours of the grounds.

To get to Tim Murphy's imposing grave, take I-88 as your starting point, exit at Route 30-Schoharie. Travel south exactly ten miles and you will come to Middleburgh Cemetery, off Hunters Land Road. Take the cemetery road all the way to the top and you will find the Murphy plot (across from the large FOSTER monument). The view from Murphy's grave is stunning. You can see ten miles in each direction and you will have an "artist's view" of the famous Vroman's Nose, a most unusual natural phenomenon that is the signature landmark of Schoharie County. The Murphy grave is marked by a plaque that reads, "TIM MURPHY. Patriot. Soldier. Scout. Citizen who served distinguishably in Morgan's Rifle Corps. Fought at Saratoga and Monmouth and whose bravery repelled the attack of the British and their Indian allies from Middlefort, October 17, 1780, and saved the lives of the colonists of his Schoharie Valley. Here too, this warrior sire, with honor rests. Who braved in freedom's cause his valiant breast."

Author's note: Schoharie County is a gorgeous region of New York State. Trips to this locale in the autumn afford the visitor an abundance of natural beauty, a treasure chest of craft and flea markets, and a cornucopia of garden vegetable stands and pumpkin patches. The Old Stone Fort (built as a church in 1772 and turned into a fort in 1780) stands as the town's most historic icon. The Battle of Schoharie was fought here, when eight hundred loyalists and Indians attacked the valley. Cannonball dents can still be seen in the stone walls of the fort. Inside is a museum with period artifacts and reading material of the people (including Tim Murphy) and events of historic Schoharie County. The Old Stone Fort also houses America's oldest fire engine, "Old Deluge." It is located at 145 Fort Road (Route 30A) on the edge of the village. For exhibits, battle reenactments, and events, call The Old Stone Fort at 518-295-7192. It is open May through October.

THE WARD BOYS

"My Brother's Keeper"

Bill, Delbert, Lymon, and Roscoe Ward are the least likely movie stars you will ever find. They were elderly brothers, illiterate and dirt poor, who shared the same two-room shanty with each other for their entire lives. Their shack had no running water, no indoor toilet, and no heat. They slept in pairs. They changed their clothes only a couple of times a year. They tended their small field and had a few chickens, which they kept in an abandoned school bus. They had a small TV and took great pleasure in watching Andy Griffith's show *Matlock*. They were filthy, forgotten, and completely happy. They lived in the threadbare farming community of Munnsville in Madison County, New York. There are approximately four hundred residents in the town. Nobody ever paid much attention to the Ward boys until one of them, Bill, turned up dead in his bed on June 5, 1990.

The death of one of the Ward boys would have slipped by unnoticed if the big city prosecutors hadn't moved in and arrested Bill's brother (and bedmate) Delbert for his murder. Although the death was originally listed as "natural," a case was built against poor Delbert that included everything, it seemed, but the proverbial kitchen sink. Was it a mercy killing? Was it a sex crime? Was it murder? Euthanasia? Revenge? Delbert insisted he did not kill his brother, but after a lengthy interrogation by the New York State Police he signed a confession saying he had covered his brother's nose and mouth and suffocated him. Nobody believed him.

Eventually the town, once so distant to the brothers, roused from its slumber and came roaring to Delbert's defense. Accusing the authorities of everything from political retribution to a land-grab deal (the Ward boys' land was small and hardscrabble but in a lucrative location), the town rallied to the brothers' cause. The good citizens of Munnsville raised $10,000 to pay for Delbert's bail and legal defense. The brothers, confused and bewildered by the fuss, remained isolated on their farm as publicity and national news coverage came calling.

A trial was held.

Author's note: I realize that the final line of this entry seems so, well, *unfinal.*

It is meant to be so. A movie documentary of the Ward boys' travails was filmed by Joe Berlinger and Bruce Sinofsky and titled *Brother's Keeper.* It was released in 1992. The film tells of the trial of Delbert Ward and its outcome, and as in the case of any whodunit, I just don't have the heart to reveal the ending to you in this book. *Brother's Keeper* is one of the most successful documentaries ever made. It was named on more than fifty critics' lists of the ten best movies of 1992. It won the New York Film Critic's Circle Award for Best Documentary. It was voted the Audience Favorite at the Sundance Film Festival. The National Board of Review named it the Best Documentary of 1992. It was a major box office success.

I profess to NOT being a film critic, but I would like to share my own ideas about the film. It is riveting and breathless in a slow-paced manner, if that is possible. The confidence that was gained by the filmmakers, which allowed them to get so close to the brothers over a nine-month filming period, is remarkable. In their childlike naiveté, the elderly brothers emerge as simple, almost reverential figures. The footage of the daily rural routine in small-town America is quite revealing in its simplicity. From the filming of a pig slaughter to the panoramic vistas of barren, forlorn farmlands in winter to the interior shots of the decrepit garbage-strewn living quarters of the Ward home, the film is shocking in its probe of life perhaps *not* as we know it. The supporting characters are well defined, especially the rallying townsfolk and the cool professional prosecuting attorneys. The film is a marvel. And I'll leave you with one last note about *Brother's Keeper.* The scene (actual local news footage) of the trial is unrelenting. Each brother takes the stand to answer questions about what happened on June 5, 1990. No Spielberg production or Tom Hanks performance could equal the reality of what you witness. The scene where one of the brothers has a nervous breakdown on the witness stand is about as much as any viewer can take. The movie is a masterpiece.

Bill Ward is buried in Stockbridge Cemetery in Munnsville. The cemetery is located on NYS Route 46, a mile north of the "S" turn in the village, off Route 33. Enter the northernmost cemetery entrance and proceed all the way to the rear of the cemetery past the flagpole. In Section K you will see a large gravestone, which marks the final resting place (now and in the future) of all of the brothers. Some are dead and some are not. Each name carries a birth and (where applicable) death date. The stone, in large letters, identifies them by the moniker they were known by for more than six decades, The Ward Boys.

SUSAN B. ANTHONY

"Failure Is Impossible"

Susan Brownell Anthony was born on February 15, 1820, in Adams, Massachusetts. She was the second of eight children born into a strict Quaker family. Her father, Daniel, believed in total dedication from his children, but not necessarily to reading and writing. His hand came down heavily on self-discipline, moral integrity, a principled lifestyle, and a zeal for justice and equality for all. Young Susan taught herself to read and write by the age of three and was home-schooled thereafter. Her private teacher was Miss Mary Perkins, and it was through Perkins that a young, growing Anthony would gain her confidence and independence. After all, Perkins was a rarity ... a female teacher in a "man's profession." Anthony progressed through her education and became a teacher herself in several different schools before settling in the Rochester, New York, area.

Anthony's Quaker parents were activists in many of the various social movements of the era. Early anti-slavery proponents, it was not unlikely to find the great abolitionist leaders of the day spending

Sunday afternoons at the Anthony home for dinner and deep discussions, with Frederick Douglass, Gerrit Smith, and William Lloyd Garrison among the frequent guests. Anthony initially took up the crusade for temperance (since alcohol was considered sinful by her religion), but found that because of her gender her voice went unheard. She moved into the anti-slavery movement, where she was vociferous in her opinions. In 1856, she became an official agent for the American Anti-Slavery Society. She leafleted, orated, rallied, and organized all across New York State. Still she was vilified by many as a female "buttinski," and saw herself hung in effigy during a speech near Syracuse. Later, the likeness was pulled down from the pole and dragged through the streets to much cheering from the onlookers. In frustration, she turned to the women's rights movement, believing that ultimately, for women to have any influence in their own lives at all, they must have the legal right to vote.

Reformist Amanda Bloomer (who created the controversial pants-like feminist garb known as "bloomers") introduced Anthony to the leader of the then-blossoming women's rights movement, Elizabeth Cady Stanton. They formed a steely union and a warm friendship that would last more than fifty years. They co-published a feminist newspaper called *The Revolution In Rochester*. Its masthead carried this declaration: "Men, their rights and nothing more; Women, their rights, and nothing less."

If Stanton was the "voice" of the movement, Anthony was certainly the "face" of it. While the cerebral and "grandmotherly" Stanton was content to express the movement's concerns and demands through her prolific writings, firebrand Anthony traveled tirelessly all over the country speaking out against the unjustness of inequality for women. She was arrested several times and was headline fodder from Wyoming to Virginia. All the while she was insisting that Congress write a constitutional amendment guaranteeing women the right to vote. Her decades-long fight eventually took its toll on her health, and, even though she carried an exhausting schedule of public appearances well into her eighties, the end was near. On her eighty-sixth birthday, she spoke quietly, yet fervently, to a small group of supporters in Washington, D.C. In what seemed like a summation of her life to those present, Anthony once more urged that the battle never be given up. Her last public utterance was symbolic of a life spent in defiance and moral certainty. "Failure," she told her admirers, "is impossible."

Less than one month later, Susan B. Anthony died peacefully in her home in Rochester. In one of her last acts, Anthony, who had never married, willed all of her earthly possessions to the suffragist movement.

More than 10,000 mourners passed by her flag-draped coffin at her funeral service. Much of Rochester was draped in black signifying a great loss for the city. Messages of condolence were read from around the country, including a touching letter from the president. Among those in person to speak of her life, William Lloyd Garrison II rose to acknowledge the importance of her early support for his father and the abolitionist movement; James G. Potter, mayor of Rochester, spoke on behalf of the thousands in his city who came to love and admire her; and women's rights leader Carrie Chapman Catt spoke of her great dedication to women's suffrage.

Anthony is buried in Mt. Hope Cemetery, Rochester, New York.

Author's note: Mt. Hope Cemetery is one of the largest and most historic cemeteries in Upstate New York. It is located at 719 Mount Hope Avenue and is several city blocks in size containing more than 450,000 burials. The main office will gladly give you a map of the famous graves found here (716-473-2755). Susan B. Anthony's is marked with arrows showing you the way to it, in Section C, Lot 93. Frederick Douglass (also in this book) is buried in this cemetery as well.

Many awards and accolades came Anthony's way, most after her death in 1906. She was featured on a U.S. postage stamp by herself *twice*, in 1936 (three-cent stamp) and in 1955 (fifty-cent stamp). In 1979, the U.S. Mint issued a Susan B. Anthony one-dollar coin. By 1997, more than 130 million of these coins were in existence, but they soon grew out of favor with the public and were hoarded or kept in private collections. In 2000, the coin was replaced by one honoring Native American Sacajawea.

The Susan B. Anthony Home and Museum is located at 17 Madison Street, Rochester (518-235-6124). It has many revolving exhibits and displays, and many personal effects from her life.

Early in the twentieth century, a massive seven-ton statue honoring the pioneers of the women's rights movement was commissioned and executed. Originally to be displayed in the Capitol Rotunda in Washington, D.C., it was deemed too unwieldy and cumbersome to be placed there (although many thought it was just simply too ugly). The official title of the tribute is "The Portrait Monument," and it features the likenesses of Susan B. Anthony, Lucretia Mott, and Elizabeth Cady Stanton "rising" out of a massive marble base. It was soon dubbed "3 Women in a Tub" and relegated to an obscure position in the Crypt of the Capitol. In 1997, Congress approved the moving of the monument to the more hallowed Rotunda to join the statuary tributes to George Washington, Thomas Jefferson, Martin Luther King, Jr., Abraham Lincoln, and others. A team of movers labored for two days to engineer the statue up from the Crypt to the next-floor Rotunda. They moved the giant statue along on tiny rollers and only cleared the stairway by four inches! The cost of moving "The Portrait Monument" to its new home was $75,000. But the ordeal for the "3 Women in a Tub" was not over yet. Congress had deemed that only eleven great tributes would be in the Rotunda at any one time, and that meant that somebody had to go. Citizens of Rhode Island pitched a fit when the decision was finally made to move ol' Roger Williams, the state's founder, into the Crypt only to be replaced by three very stern-looking feminists!

On August 18, 1920, when Kentucky became the thirty-sixth state to ratify the right to vote for all women, the 19th Amendment to the Constitution, often referred to as "Susan's Amendment," became the law of the land.

Jedediah Peck

"New York's 'Father of Education'"

In the latter part of the 1700s, formal education was still a dream far over the horizon for our fledgling nation. Oh sure, there were some pockets of enlightenment, and even some universities, but for the most part coming up with a practical, workable, sensible, and fair system of education was still a great challenge. That Jedediah Peck, an unknown, uneducated farmer from Connecticut, would lead the way to New York's groundbreaking system of education is still an incredible story.

Peck, a large, disheveled, one-eyed itinerant, came to rural Upstate New York in 1790 and settled in the newly carved out town of Burlington, just west of Cooperstown. The dominant political figure of the day was the great Judge William Cooper, a leader of the Federalist Party. In a time of landed gentry and American aristocracy, the Coopers of Cooperstown were a force to be reckoned with. Peck, however, clearly from the "other side" of the political and economic spectrum, was a man of considerable charm and persuasion, and defiantly ran against the "Cooper machine" for public office. He won on his second attempt and entered the New York State Assembly in 1798. Once in Albany, he championed social issues and sponsored forward-thinking legislation on an array of issues, ranging from personal freedoms to farming regulations to education reform. He served six years in the Assembly and four years in the New York Senate.

His feud with Judge Cooper was one of the great political sideshows of the time. Cooper, a man of great means, influence, and style, would find himself on a number of occasions stifled by the actions of his "country bumpkin" neighbor to the west. The most memorable confrontation came in 1798, and it had national implications. Cooper long heralded the Alien and Sedition Acts as a way of "checking" unpatriotic behavior. This sweeping, draconian law made it illegal to propose acts or utter defaming words against our country. Obviously, the interpretation of this law swayed to the whims of those in power. Peck, then the town supervisor of the Town of Burlington, lobbied against the acts, and Cooper had him arrested. Dramatically, Judge Cooper ordered Peck shackled in chains and transported to New York City for trial. In those days, the two-hundred-mile trip from Otsego County to New York City would normally take up to a week to traverse. During this time, the public humiliation of a "champion of the people" and an honored war veteran (he served four years in the American Revolutionary Army) was enough to fire up Peck's defenders, and they rallied for him in person and in the press. By the time Peck arrived in New York City, the scandal was full-blown and Cooper dropped the charges. Many believe that this action caused the denouement of the Federalist Party, and the great conservatives of the day, like Judge Cooper, gradually began to lose favor with the voters.

Peck's life was filled with personal hardships, having lost his entire family (parents and four siblings) to disease by the time he was twenty-three. He was basically uneducated, having studied only a few years in a small country school before dropping out. Still his passion for education was unbridled. He taught himself to read by reading the Bible every day for years. He encouraged young people to pursue higher education in almost every public speech he gave. And his time in Albany was spent working untiringly for the establishment of a common, useful school system in New York State.

In 1811, three years after he retired from public office, Governor Daniel Tompkins paid tribute to Peck's lifelong interest in New York's schools by naming him chairman of a five-man commission to study the problems and promise of the state's public school system. Having studied at a one-room schoolhouse himself, Peck was determined that there be, by official edict, a schoolhouse "within walking distance of every child's home in New York State." In 1812, the Peck Commission's suggestions were made into law. Among the law's components were the establishment of official school districts in each of the state's towns and that local taxes were to be raised to support each school district (the first school tax).

Peck was hailed as the "Father of the Common School System" in New York. He was not, however, around to hear the accolades of his peers. In 1812, at the age of *sixty-five* he re-enlisted into the army! He served heroically at the Battle of Queenston Heights.

Peck died on August 15, 1821, at the age of seventy-four, and is buried in Burlington, New York.

Author's note: While Albany Rural Cemetery and Forest Lawn in Buffalo are the largest cemeteries featured in this book, Peck's burial spot is surely in one of the smallest. In fact, it is just a small outcropping of gravestones alongside a country road. Called the Sill Farm Cemetery, it is located on NYS Route 80 just nine miles west of Cooperstown. More specifically, it is 1.6 miles east of the junction of Routes 80 and 205 in the Town of Burlington, Otsego County. A few related family members join this important figure in this largely overlooked graveyard. Only a New York State historical marker at the roadside denotes this as the final resting place of a truly remarkable man. Peck's grave marker reads, "In memory of Jedediah Peck, a Revolutionary War hero, who died Aug. 15, 1821, in the 74th year of his age. The annals of the State bear witness of his public usefulness and the recollection of his virtues bear testimony of his private work." The few other stones are very old but worthy of a few moments of exploration. One in particular, that of Giles H. Tiffany, is quite poignant. "Here lies Giles Tiffany. Died age 7 in 1842. A lovely child, a blooming boy; a father's pride and a mother's joy." Of course it is quite remarkable to see *two* veteran's markers in front of Peck's grave. One is for the American Revolution and one is for the War of 1812. This writer has never seen such a combination before.

An interesting side-trip, just down the road from the Sill Farm Cemetery, is also quite revealing. Just a mile down Route 80 (toward Cooperstown), at the corner of Bresee Road, stands a beautifully restored *bright red* one-room schoolhouse. And situated so close to the grave of the man who probably made such a school possible! In the yard beside this schoolhouse is an intriguing granite marker. It is worth reading the lengthy text, which recalls the land's ancestors and their beginnings in Upstate New York. The marker bears a heading reading "They Faced Life Bravely." It can be seen clearly from the road.

SAM PATCH

"The Yankee Leaper"

Sam Patch is one of the greatest legends of Upstate New York.

Famed as a daredevil jumper (the "Evel Kneivel" of his day), Patch would jump off just about any precipice around if the publicity was plentiful, the check was for the right money, and the crowd was big enough. He made his first jump in September of 1827 from the heights of the Passaic Palisades. This seventy-foot leap was unheard of, and news of his feat quickly made him one of the more curious "stars" of his era. Next he jumped off a one-hundred-foot platform over Niagara Falls, the first to ever do so and live to tell about it!

His next challenge was the raging whitewaters spilling over the Genesee River in Rochester, New York. On November 6, 1829, he leaped into the foaming river with his pet bear in his arms! When he (and the bear) emerged from the water safely, he was hailed as the greatest jumper in history. One week later, he attempted the same jump in front of a huge crowd (this time without the bear!) and failed. The crowd stood in stunned silence as they waited for Sam Patch to come to the water's surface. His body was found four months later. Perhaps he should have taken into consideration the date of his fateful, and final, jump: *Friday the 13th*, 1829. He was twenty-two years old when he died.

Sam Patch is buried in Charlotte Cemetery, near Rochester, New York.

Author's note: Patch's gravesite is very easily found. Charlotte Cemetery is at River and Lake Streets in Charlotte, New York, a suburb of Rochester, right across the street from the Charlotte Fire Department. His large gravestone can be easily seen from the street. The historical marker at the site reads, "The grave of SAM PATCH who leaped to his death over the upper falls of the Genesee River at Rochester on Friday, November 13, 1829. His remains were found in the lower part of the Genesee River on March 17, 1839 and interred in this cemetery." Perhaps the definitive biography of Patch is the exciting-to-read *Sam Patch-The Famous Jumper* (Hill and Wang) by author Paul E. Johnson. Sam Patch was one of the first inductees into the Daredevil Hall of Fame, where he is joined by other jumpers, barrel riders, acrobats, and flyers who have braved death near the mouth of Niagara Falls (including Annie Taylor, the first "barrel jumper" to survive a trip over the falls, and who is featured in this book). The Hall of Fame is located at 5651 River Road at Hwy 420, Niagara Falls, Ontario, Canada. In the gift shop, you may purchase a vintage-style broadside advertisement depicting Sam Patch's "Great Leap." Admission is free. For events and hours, call 716-285-4898 (www.daredevilhalloffame.com).

An interesting copycat story takes us to the saga of a Japanese seaman who also had a bit of "daredevil" in him and was referred to as the "Japanese Sam Patch." Going by the nickname "Senta," he made a name for himself both in his country and ours. He was the only Japanese to accompany Perry on his expedition to open Japan, the first Japanese to enroll at Colgate University, the first Japanese to serve in the U.S. Navy, and the first Japanese to be baptized as a Baptist!

KATE SMITH

"God Bless America!"

The parents of little Kathryn Smith were duly alarmed when she still had not spoken a word by her fourth birthday. Specialists were sought and treatments considered. Finally, halfway through her fourth year, little Kate started to talk—and didn't stop for seventy-five years!

Endowed with a disarming naturalness and a much-envied singing voice, she would become one of the most famous women in the world with tens of millions of admirers. And it is through singing (and talking) that Kate Smith found her way into America's history books. By her twenty-first birthday, she had already become one of the nation's most popular entertainers. Her legendary career would span half of the twentieth century and set standards for excellence and professionalism rarely seen today.

After beginning her career as a featured Broadway singer and dancer, where her three-hundred-pound frame was the source of biting and hateful remarks from co-stars jealous of her voice and magnetic appeal, Kate Smith was "saved" by the powerful influence of her newfound friend and manager, Ted Collins. Together they formed the Kated Corporation, still the most successful show-business merger in history. Take *that*, Elvis and Colonel Parker!

Ted fashioned Kate into the greatest star of the earliest days of radio (where she could be heard rather than seen), earning her more than $18,000 *per week* by the age of twenty-three. Millions tuned in each week to hear her familiar and folksy signature lines, "Hello, everybody!" and "Thanks for listenin'." Her songs sold by the millions all across the heartland of Depression America. She was responsible for introducing an astonishing six hundred new songs during her radio career. During her lifetime, she introduced more than three thousand songs, still more than any other performer. She was said to have had a magical intuition about which songs would become hits, and the list is awesome, from "When the Moon Comes over the Mountain" (her self-penned theme song) to "God Bless America."

She also introduced several lasting stars on her radio program, most notably Abbott and Costello. During Word War II, Kate was a tireless supporter of the War Bond effort and is personally responsible for selling over 600 million dollars' worth of bonds. Deemed too valuable to the American patriotic spirit to be put in harm's way overseas, Kate instead visited hundreds of airbases, hospitals, and veterans' groups from coast to coast.

Kate probably earned her everlasting niche in American history when she triumphantly introduced Irving Berlin's immortal "God Bless America" on her radio show on Armistice Day, 1938. It quickly became the nation's second national anthem, and Kate had to personally persuade Congress not to replace the "Star Spangled Banner" with *her* song as our country's anthem. She suggested that because the anthem was written while our country was at war (War of 1812) it was more suitable as a national symbol.

One remarkable footnote to her biography is that so appealing was this great lady to the masses of fans that she became the first great female star of *both* of the twentieth century's great mediums, radio and television. She starred in the first popular entertainment and talk show in 1950, during television's infancy. She would be a welcome and frequent guest on TV over the next twenty-five years.

A familiar figure to four generations of Americans, Kate Smith was reported to have received more fan mail than any other celebrity (the *New York Times* put the figure at fifteen million letters!) and several times was voted one of the three most important women in the world. She was given our nation's ultimate honor, the Medal of Freedom, by President Ronald Reagan shortly before her death.

The Greenville, Virginia, native had a home in Lake Placid, New York, for the last forty years of her life. Her final years were marked with harrowing health problems, including brain damage and amputations due to diabetes. She died on June 17, 1986, exactly ten years to the day of her last public appearance. Millions felt they had lost a best friend.

Kate is buried in a huge pink mausoleum in St. Agnes Cemetery, at the corner of Sentinel and Cascade Roads in Lake Placid. It is one of the most visited sights of the Adirondack region.

Author's note: More than a year's worth of wrangling took place before Kate was finally interred at St. Agnes. The church, which was the major beneficiary of Kate's estate, had never allowed a mausoleum of the type she had wished for in her will. She had always been afraid of "going underground" and explicitly directed her estate managers to have an above-the-ground mausoleum constructed for her. After a year of withering bad press and inquests by her fans and admirers all across the country, the church finally relented, and Kate's beautiful pink marble tomb was built. If you look inside the glass door of the mausoleum, you will see, directly under the stained-glass window, a beautiful photo of Kate smiling. On the wall are inscribed the words of FDR, "This is Kate Smith. This is America!" Kate's biography, *When the Moon Comes over the Mountain*, by Richard K. Hayes (McFarland Publishing), was printed in 1995, and The Kate Smith Commemorative Society, an offshoot of her longtime fan club, is one of the most active of its kind. In fact, each year, a great crowd of Kate's fans and friends gather in Lake Placid for a joyous festival dedicated to her life, her music, and her spirit (www.katesmith.org).

Ezra Cornell

"High Above Cayuga's Waters..."

Among the rolling foothills of Western New York, at the edge of the Wine Region, and high above the shores of Cayuga Lake stands a sprawling monument to a great man of vision and generosity, an internationally honored university that bears his name. The man was Ezra Cornell.

Cornell was born in Westchester, New York, grew up in rural DeRuyter, and lived in Ithaca from 1828 until his death in 1874. As a lifelong resident of Upstate New York, he saw many opportunities become available to him, and he grabbed every one of them. He was a successful farmer, businessman, and financier, although much of his fame and fortune came after his fiftieth birthday.

After securing a comfortable niche for himself in the upper echelons of Ithaca society, he turned his energies to inventing and toward his interest in the new field of telegraphy. Cornell invented the single most important piece of machinery (a "trench-digger" first, then a unique way to erect and string up telegraph poles and wires) that enabled Samuel F.B. Morse to successfully lay the first telegraph line from Washington, D.C., to Baltimore, and it made him a rich man. It was Cornell's wires that carried Morse's famous first telegraph message on May 24, 1844, "What hath God wrought?" He immersed himself in the frenetic development of telegraph lines throughout the expanding countryside. New York, Washington, Baltimore, Quebec, Detroit, Chicago, Kansas City, and all points west soon saw the familiar lines of Cornell's telegraph systems. Joining his largest competitor, Hiram Sibley of the New York & Mississippi Valley Printing Telegraph Company, Cornell founded and led the newly named Western Union Company in 1855. For fifteen years, Cornell was the largest stockholder of this new company and earned millions (in 1850s dollars!) from his investments.

Once at a stage where money was no longer the great driving factor in his life, he devoted his passion and his vast fortune to the development of a seat of higher education to be located in his beloved Ithaca. He gave $500,000 and a large tract of land to be used as the site of a great university bearing his name. The school opened in 1868.

He was always extremely proud, in a patriarchal way, of Cornell University. In his autumnal years, he lived on campus and became a familiar sight wandering the halls and lawns of his college, mingling with the students.

From the Western Union Company to the establishment of a great university, Ezra Cornell's influence was a vital component in the growth of our nation in the nineteenth century. His legacy lived on through his children, too, and his offspring included son Alonzo Cornell, who was elected governor of New York in 1880.

Cornell died in 1874, and in accordance with his wish, he was buried on campus. The Sage Chapel is a building of quiet majesty, and in a room near the front you will find the marble sarcophagi of Cornell and his wife, the former Mary Ann Wood. The details of the funerary sculptures are so real that you can count the pleats in old Ezra's pants!

Author's note: Ithaca is a thriving community of 30,000 people. The city is a wonderful blend of international excitement (from the many foreign students in the area) and modernity, combined with all the traditional small-town nuances (after all, the ice cream sundae was invented in Ithaca at Platt's Drugstore in 1892). Nestled along the bucolic shoreline of one of the largest of New York's Finger Lakes, the city is dominated by the physical and spiritual presence of the sprawling university campus and its thousands of students. Signs at virtually every corner will direct you to the college. When you visit Sage Chapel to view the final resting place of the university's founder, spend a few reflective moments absorbing the historic building. It is a place of quiet serenity at the hub of a vital and electric campus. It also houses a very rare Aeolian-Skinner grand organ with nearly four thousand pipes! A tour of the campus, arranged by the admissions office, will also direct you to the towering statue of Ezra Cornell, created by famed sculptor Herman Atkins MacNeil, in the center of the Arts Quad. The renowned Herbert Johnson Museum of Art is nearby. This museum, designed by I.M. Pei in 1973, is reportedly on the exact site where Ezra is said to have announced to the world his intention of founding a great university!

SAMUEL WILSON

"The REAL Uncle Sam!"

Samuel Wilson is a man whose concocted image is as vivid to all Americans as perhaps any other symbol. Regardless of what he *actually* looked like, we eternally envision him as a tall, lanky man with a white, wispy beard. His sleeves are usually rolled up, and he is determinedly standing up for America. Almost always he is dressed in his familiar red, white, and blue suit and tall top hat. Yes, Samuel Wilson *is* America!

Well, maybe.

The real "Uncle Sam" was born Samuel Wilson in Mason, New Hampshire. After serving as a drummer in the Revolutionary War, Sam and his brother Ebenezer *walked* west from New Hampshire to Troy, New York, where they went into the meatpacking business. By the time the next great war came along, the War of 1812, Sam Wilson was one of the leading meat procurers in the Northeast. It has been handed down through the years that Wilson would stamp his meat barrels with "US" for United States. One time, a contingent of military contractors visited Wilson's meatpacking plant in Troy and, with tongue in cheek, asked a worker what the "US" stood for. Put on the spot, the worker replied, "Uncle Sam!" his hard-working, honest, and reliable boss. The story stuck, and thus, the legend of "Uncle Sam" was born.

It wasn't until one of America's foremost cartoonists drew up the now-iconic image of Uncle Sam that the myth really took off. James Montgomery Flagg was the first to depict the familiar figure of "Uncle Sam"/America. Flagg placed him on the cover of the popular *Leslie's Weekly Magazine* on July 6, 1916, featuring a story titled "What Are You Doing For Preparedness?" This became the well-known "I Want You" army recruitment poster, and between 1917 and 1919, four million posters were sold. Flagg called it "the most famous poster in the world." Later it was taken out of mothballs for World War II, and the poster again was extremely popular. When Flagg presented an original copy to President Franklin D. Roosevelt and told him the story of how the artist had been so broke when he drew it that he used himself as a model to save on modeling fees, FDR replied, "I congratulate you on your resourcefulness, Mr. Flagg. By saving on your modeling hire, your method suggests our Yankee forbearers."

In a nation so steeped in symbolism, it is a rare treat to be able to actually go and visit a gravesite of one who inspired such a symbol. While we all know that there really *was* a Paul Revere and a Betsy Ross, it is also important to know that there was a "real" Uncle Sam and that he is honored with a memorial at his grave in Troy. And how do we separate the "real" from the "myth"? Well, let's let Congress sort it out for us. On September 15, 1961, this notice was entered in the Congressional Record: "Resolved by the Senate and the House of Representatives that the Congress unanimously salutes Uncle Sam Wilson of Troy, N.Y., as the progenitor of America's National Symbol of 'Uncle Sam'."

Author's note: His grave is one of the most visited of any in Upstate New York. Small signs directing the way to "Uncle Sam's

Grave" denote the short distance from the entrance of Oakwood Cemetery to his actual site. A large brass commemorative plaque telling his story and a flagpole mark the spot. A local Boy Scout troop raises the flag at this site every day. Obviously, Troy celebrates this story with great relish. Throughout Troy you will find "Uncle Sam" diners, laundromats, and florists in great abundance. In fact, greeting visitors driving over the Hudson River into the city, you will see signs saying, "Welcome to Troy! The Home of Uncle Sam!" This slogan resonates much more sentimentally than the city's previous one, "Collar City." Despite the fact that the city was the birthplace of the detachable shirt collar, the Chamber of Commerce eventually saw the more favorable aesthetic value of having Uncle Sam as a city image rather than a starched shirt accessory!

Oakwood Cemetery is located on Oakwood Avenue, nearly across the street from Frear Park in Troy, just a mile from the bridge that carries you on NYS Route 7 (known locally as Hoosick Street) over the Hudson from Albany. Many famous Americans are buried in this historic cemetery (including Russell Sage and Captain William Van Schaick, whose entries are in this book), and it is worth an afternoon strolling the beautiful grounds with the guide map, available at the front gate, in your hands. The cemetery is enormous (thirty-two miles of roads and paths), and many interesting memorials can be found. One in particular, the grave of Robert Ross in the E1 section, offers the most stunning vista I have ever seen in a New York cemetery. Also, don't miss the large, old crematorium building with original Tiffany stained-glass windows!

GREGORY JARVIS

"Space Shuttle Challenger"

Gregory Jarvis was born in Michigan but was raised in Upstate New York. He graduated from Mohawk Central High School in 1962 and earned a bachelor's degree from SUNY Buffalo and later a master's degree from Northeastern University in Boston. After retiring from the military, he worked for several space-related firms before joining NASA.

Jarvis was a payload specialist when he boarded the Space Shuttle *Challenger* for his first flight in space. Jarvis and the entire *Challenger* crew were killed instantly when the spacecraft exploded over the Atlantic Ocean at 11:30 AM (EST) on January 28, 1986.

Astronaut Jarvis loved physical activities, especially cycling, skiing, and playing squash. He played classical guitar to relax. His wife, Marcia, survives him. He was posthumously awarded the Congressional Space Medal of Honor.

A remembrance to Greg Jarvis is found in Mohawk Cemetery, Mohawk, New York.

Author's note: Mohawk Cemetery is on NYS Route 28 just as you enter the village. Coming from the south, make your first left-hand turn into the cemetery and proceed three-quarters of the way through. Stop here and Jarvis's grave is in the center of the section on your right.

The tragedy of the *Challenger* disaster all too vividly reminded Americans that our pursuit of space exploration was not without a price. Greg Jarvis's marker (on the back face of his family's gravestone) is a poignant tribute to a quiet man from small-town America who, as President Reagan described, "slipped the surly bonds of earth and touched the face of God." A large color photograph of a smiling Astronaut Jarvis adorns the small monument.

The burial places of other American space pioneers are as follows (in some instances, no remains were found and grave markers act as memorials only).

Space Shuttle *Challenger* (January 28, 1986)

S. Christa McAuliffe ("First Teacher in Space"), Calvary Cemetery, Concord, New Hampshire

Ronald McNair, Rest Lawn Cemetery, Lake City, South Carolina

Dr. Judith Resnik, Arlington Cemetery, Virginia

Francis Dick Scobee, Arlington Cemetery, Virginia (Section #46)

Michael J. Smith, Arlington Cemetery, Virginia (Section 7A)

Ellison Onizuka, National Memorial Cemetery of the Pacific, Honolulu, Hawaii

Space Shuttle *Columbia* (February 1, 2003)

Rick Husband, Llano Cemetery, Amarillo, Texas

Ilan Ramon, Israel

Willie McCool, U.S. Naval Academy Cemetery, Annapolis, Maryland

Michael Anderson, Arlington Cemetery, Virginia (Section #46)

David Brown, Arlington Cemetery, Virginia (Section #46)

Laurel Clark, Arlington Cemetery, Virginia (Section #46)

Kalpana Chawla, cremated

Apollo capsule fire (January 27, 1967)

Virgil "Gus" Grissom, Arlington Cemetery, Virginia (Section 3)

Edward H. White, U.S. Military Academy Post Cemetery, West Point, New York

Roger B. Chafee, Arlington Cemetery, Virginia (Section 3)

B. F. GOODRICH

"The Rubber King"

Benjamin Goodrich started out wanting to be a doctor. He would have been the first to tell you that he knew nothing about rubber or tires. In the end, however, his name would become synonymous with both.

He began studying medicine at the age of seventeen and went on to have a short, yet distinguished, career as a surgeon. During the Civil War, he served as a field surgeon with the Army of the Potomac. He moved to far western New York State (Jamestown) after the war and soon grew uninterested in the tiring routine of doctoring and finally just abandoned it as a career. He got involved in the lucrative real-estate market in New York City with a friend and soon amassed a small fortune. He did this before he reached thirty.

On speculation, the two friendly investors purchased a large rubber manufacturing plant, paying $5,000 for everything. Goodrich knew very little about the industry but sensed a great and growing potential for it down the road (pun intended). He nurtured his investment wisely, researched his product extensively, created innovative marketing strategies, and became more and more involved in the potential of rubber.

On December 31, 1870, he established a new company in Akron, Ohio. It seems that the city officials of Akron, frantic for new capital to come to their struggling city, had invited Goodrich to come and view the possibilities. Always a salesman, he turned his powers of persuasion on "full throttle" to the city fathers, and within forty-eight hours of his arrival in Akron, not only had he made a commitment to relocate his factory there, but the community leaders actually gave *him* large sums of money to do so! "The Rubber City" was born.

The B.F. Goodrich Company was incorporated on May 10, 1888, and became one of the industrial giants of the era and the largest tire manufacturer in the world. Benjamin Goodrich died just ten weeks later, on August 3, 1888, at the age of forty-seven.

He is buried in Lake View Cemetery, Jamestown, New York.

Author's note: One would imagine that a man of B.F. Goodrich's vast wealth and stature would be buried in an imposing monument-like tomb. Not so. In fact, without the assistance of cemetery personnel, his grave was almost impossible to find. Why? Well, because Goodrich lies under a stone bearing the family name of MARVIN, his wife's name. (Perhaps this was done to allow him to rest anonymously forever, away from the prying eyes of people like me.) There, along with a whole host of Marvins, you will find the small, twelve-inch headstone bearing the inscription "Benjamin F. Goodrich. Nov. 4, 1841–Aug. 3, 1888." The grave is located in the Highland Section, in the center of the old part of the cemetery about three hundred yards in from the Buffalo Street entrance. A tall monument bearing the name MARVIN is easily spotted. Lakeview Cemetery is located at 90 Lakeview Street (716-665-3206).

Other famous gravesites include those of former New York State Senator Charles Goodell, an early Vietnam critic, and former New York Governor Reuben Fenton (1865–69). Also, three members of the famed Excelsior Brigade, whose fourteen members *each* received the Congressional Medal of Honor for action during the Civil War, are buried here. They are Major Edgar Pierpont Putnam, whose grave is located just inside the Buffalo Street entrance to the right of the giant Prendergast monument; Sgt. Henry L. Brown, whose grave is located one hundred feet behind Putnam's; and Pvt. James M. Youngs, buried fifty feet from Brown. Maj. Putnam's grave is the only one to carry the Medal of Honor plaque on it. The grave of James Prendergast (yes, he is the founding *James* of *James*town) is one of the most incredible in size and stature of any this author has seen. Lucille Ball is also buried in Lake View (see her entry in this book). The graves of Goodrich, Prendergast, and Ball are all within view of each other.

The history of automobiles in America is filled with legendary names. Goodrich put the tires on their cars, but where did the automakers eventually end up? Some of them are buried in New York, some are not. Here is a short list with their burial places:

Preston T. Tucker, Michigan Memorial Park, Flat Rock, Michigan
Louis Chevrolet, Holy Cross and Saint James Cemetery, Indianapolis
Henry Ford, Ford Family Cemetery, Joy Road, Detroit, Michigan
Walter Chrysler, Sleepy Hollow Cemetery, Tarrytown, New York
Ranson E. Olds, Mount Hope Cemetery, Lansing, Michigan
John and Henry Dodge, Woodlawn Cemetery, Detroit, Michigan
James Packard, Cleveland Memorial Cemetery, Lansing, Michigan
Charles Nash, Forest Lawn Park, Glendale, California
Harvey Firestone, Columbiana Cemetery, Akron, Ohio
Charles Duryea (maker of first auto), Ivy Hill Cemetery, Philadelphia
Clem Studebaker, Riverview Cemetery, South Bend, Indiana
John Z. DeLorean, White Chapel Cemetery, Troy, Michigan
William Durant (General Motors), Woodlawn Cemetery, Bronx, New York

MATTHEW VASSAR

"The Brewer Philanthropist"

Matthew Vassar started out in life to be a beer-maker. His father ran a successful brewery in Poughkeepsie, New York, and when it burned to the ground in 1822, young Matthew built a new one. It became a highly profitable endeavor for him and quickly made him a very rich young man. But, although he would be involved in the brewery business for nearly a half-century, the source of his everlasting fame would come from a much different source (albeit one that was funded with "beer money"), the field of women's education.

Vassar enjoyed spreading his wealth around. A curious investor, he provided the seed money for his nephew's efforts to settle and develop the new territory that we now know as the state of Michigan. The town of Vassar, Michigan, stands even today as a proud tribute to the fruits of his investment.

He also invested heavily in the whaling industry and eventually built one of the largest whaling docks of the time. It was during this income-amassing period of his life that Vassar chose to turn his financial energies to a more socially responsible area. His young niece, Miss Lydia Booth, had been the headmistress at an all-girl school in Poughkeepsie and it was through his association with her that Vassar charted the establishment of a school for the higher education of women.

In 1861, he donated the land and nearly a half-million dollars toward the building of Vassar College. With an illustrious board of trustees that included Samuel F. B. Morse and Henry Ward Beecher, Vassar College quickly grew into the model of its kind in the nation. Faced with strong competition from older, more entrenched female schools, Vassar College soon found itself fighting for each and every student and eventually had to turn to its founder for help. In what would be an innovative new tactic, Vassar decided to advertise his college (the first institution of its kind to do so) in hopes of attracting worldwide recognition for his sprawling new campus in the Hudson Valley. This startling new marketing ploy worked, and in no time, Vassar College became the most popular and successful women's college in America. In the words of his niece, Lydia Booth, "Vassar College stands proudly as a monument more lasting than the Great Pyramids."

The oft-told campus legend recalls that on the morning of June 23, 1868, Vassar uncharacteristically went out and splurged on a shiny new three-piece suit for himself. He was attending an important Board of Trustees meeting at the college and, despite being more than seventy-five years old, wanted to make an impression with his colleagues. As the meeting ended, Vassar reached into his vest pocket and pulled out a slip of paper from which he began to read. It was an announcement of his final retirement from the College Board after decades of tireless service. When he had finished his speech, he silently sat back down in his chair, put his head down on the table, and died of a massive heart attack. He was buried three days later in his shiny new three-piece suit.

After a large funeral at the First Baptist Church of Poughkeepsie (a church also built with his "beer money"), Matthew Vassar was laid to rest next to his wife, Catherine. Today his gravestone is readily recognizable from the many others in Poughkeepsie Rural Cemetery. It is in the shape of the ancient symbol of knowledge, a four-foot-tall acorn!

His institution of higher learning still stands today as one of the great learning centers in the country. Located seventy-five miles north of New York City, it has an enrollment of 2,400 students at the campus located at 124 Raymond Avenue. With more than two hundred different varieties of trees and shrubs beautifying its more than one thousand acres, the *entire campus* is treated as an arboretum! Vassar College (845-437-7000) was the first all-women's college to go co-educational, in 1969, and men now count for 40 percent of its enrollment.

Author's note: Poughkeepsie Rural Cemetery (845-454-6020) is located at 342 South Avenue. It is a beautiful, sprawling area dotted with glens and hills and ponds and paths. Matthew Vassar's impressive gravesite is located at Lot 17, Section L. Many other historic people are buried here, and the front office will gladly help any visitor with information. Two of the most famous "residents" are

William and Andrew Smith. They owned what was once the most recognizable company product in America: Smith Brothers cough drops. Famed for their bearded visages peering out from the front of every box, it was William who was over the word "TRADE" and Andrew over the word "MARK."

ZEBULON PIKE _____

"Pike's Peak"

Zebulon Pike was born in New Jersey, explored the far West, fought wars in Canada, was arrested by Spain for trespassing in Colorado, and is buried in New York. He certainly got around.

In 1805, he led a twenty-man party on a two-thousand-mile exploration seeking the headwaters of the Mississippi River (then uncharted). A year later, he led another expedition surveying the far-reaching borders of the newly acquired Louisiana Purchase. It was on this trip that he first saw the mountain peak in Colorado that would eventually be named after him. Despite folklore to the contrary, he never scaled Pike's Peak. Heading south, Pike and his men were arrested after straying into Spanish territory in what is today New Mexico. His party was taken deep into Spanish territory, giving him a unique look at a hitherto unseen region. His reports and published accounts illuminated the potential trading business with the Spanish and brought about a great rush to the region of Texas and the Southwest. On spying the desert areas of the West, however, he had little to comment in a positive way. He likened the American desert region to the vast deserts of Africa, and because of this, investors stayed away from the area in droves.

Pike entered the army in 1793 and rose to the rank of second lieutenant. Assigned to the large military complex on the New York/Canadian border in Sackets Harbor, Pike led several forays into Canada during the War of 1812 and was promoted to brigadier general. On April 27, 1813, Pike led an army of 1,700 men across the Great Lakes to attack York, Canada (now Toronto). The defenders threw everything they had at Pike's men, and the battle was fierce. The British, anticipating the possibility of defeat, had cunningly laid a trap for the Americans. They planted a huge minefield near their fort. They filled it with explosives and heavy boulders. They would attempt to lure the American troops into this area and set off the charge. All was going well for the British when unaccountably the minefield exploded prematurely. A horrific blast killed forty-two British soldiers and fifty-two Americans. A boulder struck Brig. Gen. Pike so severely in the back that it nearly split his spine. Lying on the battlefield as the tide turned for the Americans, legend has it that Pike called for the British colors to be struck and the American flag to be raised in victory. The British flag was brought to him and put under his head to comfort him. He died on the battlefield. He was thirty-four.

Brig. Gen. Zebulon Pike is buried in the Old Military Cemetery in Sackets Harbor, New York.

Author's note: Sackets Harbor is as close to a New England coastal community as New York has to offer. Hard on the waterfront where the St. Lawrence Seaway spills into the Great Lakes, it is an old fishing center steeped in military history. The Old Military Cemetery is in the historic part of the small town, and Pike's grave, with a large wooden shaft sticking into the air, is unmistakable. His gravestone reads, "In Memory of Gen. Z. M. Pike. Killed at York, UC 27 April 1813." The nearby Madison Barracks are restored and offer a glimpse into the military past of this town. Sackets Harbor

Battlefield is a popular destination, just thirty miles across the water from Canada. For events at the battlefield, call 315-646-3643. For other events, re-enactments, and commemorations, call the Sackets Harbor Historical Society at 315-646-1700. There is much to offer in this coastal town, and the ghosts of its past are not hard to conjure. At one time, fully half of the entire U.S. Army and one-quarter of the U.S. Navy were stationed at Sackets Harbor.

On another note, Pike and his wife, Clarissa, had several children yet all but one died at very young ages. The surviving daughter married the son of President William Henry Harrison.

Pike's Peak rises 14,110 feet out of the Colorado countryside. Long a top tourist destination in the state, it boasts the highest railroad in the nation, the Pikes Peak Cog Railway. For an amazing "cyber-view" of this mountain, visit www.pikespeak.cam.com. A live image of Pike's Peak appears on the screen every minute of the day. It is fun to watch a storm move in and over the mountain on your computer! (The camera is mounted on an office building in Colorado Springs some fifteen miles away.)

SAINTS GOUPIL,
JOGUES, AND LALANDE

"The North American Martyrs"

This entry is about America's first and only canonized martyrs. Three Jesuit missionaries, Rene Goupil, Isaac Jogues, and John LaLande, set about the virgin territory of central New York in the early 1600s to spread the word of God to the Indian tribes along the Mohawk Valley. They were courageous men of the cloth who sought only enlightenment and peace, yet they were met with suspicion, hatred, fear, and, ultimately, harrowing deaths.

Auriesville, New York, was then called Ossernenon and was the home of the nomadic Mohawk society known as the Turtle Clan. Faced with recurring disease, this clan (or community) would move often to avoid being decimated by illness. With a population of about six hundred, Ossernenon was located on a high bluff overlooking the Mohawk River (near present-day Amsterdam, New York), and it was here that the Turtles found lasting communal stability.

The Jesuits had come from New France (Canada) around 1625, and in 1642, they sent a small missionary force to Ossernenon to "bring forth the word of the Lord" to the Mohawks. Leading the small party was a young priest named Father Isaac Jogues.

Father Jogues had good intentions. He knew the Indians harbored deep suspicions toward the "black robes" (priests), but he was compelled to help them. He was en route with a canoe filled with medicines and staples when a war party swept down from the hills on August 1, 1642, and captured him and his men. A "black robe" was a high prize for a war party to catch, since many priests, while hated, were used as valuable trade with the white men for goods and land. The entire village of Ossernenon came out to meet the returning warriors and their human bounty. Many in the missionary party were killed outright, but special attention was paid to young Father Jogues. His fingernails were pulled out one by one, and warriors chewed his hands into pulp.

A young assistant to Father Jogues, Brother Rene Goupil, was the only other survivor of the original party. Brother Goupil was made to run a Mohawk gauntlet where he was pummeled with sharpened sticks. His thumbs were torn off and displayed as trophies. Despite their terrible wounds, both men were deliberately kept alive, so as to retain their "trade value."

Over a period of ten weeks in captivity, the Jesuits, although always shackled and watched, were afforded meager amounts of freedom from their Indian captors. With the supervision of a guard, they were allowed to go to a hilltop and pray. They were allowed "work times" in the village. And they were sheltered in decent living quarters. Still they knew the patience of the Mohawks was limited.

Brother Goupil was the first to die. One day, while playing with a small Indian child, he was observed making the Sign of the Cross on the child's forehead. The grandfather of the child flew into a rage and demanded that the chief kill the missionary. A short time later, while he was walking in the woods reciting the rosary, Brother Goupil was attacked and killed. The day was September 29, 1642, the Feast Day of Saint Michael.

The warriors dragged the dead body through the village and left it on display. That night, Father Jogues slipped out of his hut and recovered the remains of his friend. He pulled the body of the young man to a nearby stream and buried it in the shallow waters under a heavy mound of rocks. He quickly and quietly committed Brother Goupil's soul to God and sneaked back into camp.

Measures became more severe for the lone captive now. For thirteen long months, Father Jogues toiled in the fields of Ossernenon as a slave. The Mohawks frequently paraded him in front of traders, seeking a high ransom for the priest, but none was offered. Then his luck began to change.

In August of 1643, the Mohawks took the priest with them on a fishing mission to Albany. It was on this trip, perhaps with inspiration from his Divine Master, that Father Jogues finally plotted his escape. With the help of a sympathetic Dutch minister, the Jesuit was spirited away from the Mohawks and safely off to France, where he was received as a hero.

Popes and queens sought audience with the cleric who had suffered so much for his beliefs. He traveled extensively and wrote of his adventures in the New World. But time wore on, and this zealous missionary was soon asking to go back to Canada. The Mohawks were becoming slightly more temperate, and the opportunity for mission work appeared to be marginally less dangerous. His request was granted by his superiors, and he departed for Canada.

The social climate among the native tribes in Canada was exactly what he expected. White men and Indians were working more closely together, and the violence had subsided considerably. In this positive atmosphere, Jogues requested that he be sent back to Ossernenon, the site of his earlier travails. He felt certain that God had meant him to return there, and he had actually dreamt of establishing a permanent mission in the Mohawk Valley, a mission he would dedicate to the martyrs who had died there in the service of God. A passionate and deliberate speaker, he was able to convince his superiors to let him return to Ossernenon, but with one condition. He must be accompanied by a lay minister who would act as a buffer between the "black robe" and the Mohawks. They agreed, and John LaLande, a French aide, was chosen to go along.

Joined by friendly Huron warriors, the small party set out for Ossernenon. As fear and uncertainty about the mission grew, the Indian scouts fled the party in terror as they approached the border of the Mohawk community. Only Jogues and LaLande entered the village's gates. They would, to their horror, find out immediately that little had changed since Jogues's last visit.

War-painted Mohawks attacked the two men of peace and brought them to the Mohawk elders. Ill timing had brought the Frenchmen to the village during a period of severe drought and disease to its inhabitants. Villagers blamed the two for their plight and called for their deaths. Several Mohawks who had previously befriended Jogues pleaded for the life of their friend. It was to no avail. A howling mob screamed for blood, and Father Jogues was chosen as the first to die.

The crowd carried the priest aloft through the village paths, tearing at him in a frenzy. A ceremonial scalping was the final torture for the priest. His head was cut off and placed atop a tall spike at the entrance of the community.

The next morning, John LaLande found the headless corpse of his friend and tried to secretly bury it. He was found out and was set upon by warriors. He too was beheaded and his head strung up next to Jogues's. These macabre markers remained at the gates of the village for nearly a year.

News of the deaths of these three peaceful missionaries resonated throughout the religious world. Perhaps the irony of their story is the fact that missionary work was increased, instead of lessened, and the growth of Christianity throughout the Indian nations grew at an astonishing pace.

The three martyrs buried on the grounds of Ossernenon (Auriesville) have been the source of great study over the years. Beatification honors were bestowed upon all three (after lengthy and exhaustive investigation by the Church) on June 21, 1925. The three were canonized as "Martyrs of the Church" by Pope Pius XI on June 29, 1930. The beatification document tells of the saintly devotion and courage displayed by all three, "These Servants of God were, by nature, meek and timid, but by constant self-humiliation and the continuous practice of prayer they so strengthened their spirit … and in facing dangers and torments, gave truly marvelous examples of Christian fortitude."

"The Ravine," a natural glen on the grounds of Auriesville, holds the remains of The North American Martyrs.

Author's note: More than 75,000 visitors visit this holy site each year. Ossernenon/Auriesville is located in northern Upstate New York, along the Mohawk River. It is one of the most beautiful and inspirational places in the state. Its six hundred acres of manicured lawns and blooming gardens hold countless shrines to faith. An exact replica of the famed Pieta rests under a golden canopy. A football-field-sized rosary of white boulders marks the spot where the first rosary was said in North America. A massive "Church of 72 Doors" is an active place of worship for all denominations. Visitors come to this place from the farthest reaches of the globe to worship at the feet of a carved, four-hundred-year-old image of the Virgin Mary, one of the oldest known religious artifacts in the nation. Places of quietude, dotted with statues and sculptures, adorn the grounds. It is truly an amazing place. Tour bus groups make up a large contingent of the visitors, and there are modern dining facilities and restrooms. Gift shops sell tasteful religious items and reading material. Located forty miles west of Albany, the easiest way to access Auriesville is from the New York State Thruway. From the Amsterdam, New York, exit, many signs will point you along the five or so miles to this major visitor destination.

One other note of interest: Ossernenon is also the birthplace of Kateri Tekakwitha, who was born here in 1656, ten years after the martyrdom. Known as the "Lily of the Mohawks," Kateri is a revered religious figure and was declared a Servant of God by Pope

Pius XII on January 3, 1943. Many believe that she will become the next North American Saint. There are many displays and artifacts of Kateri's early life at The Shrine of the North American Martyrs. An interesting side trip to this religious region is The National Shrine to the Blessed Kateri Tekakwitha in Fonda, New York. This is located just east of Auriesville at Exit 28 of the New York State Thruway. This is her birthplace, and it is visited by throngs each year. She is, however, buried in Kahnawake, Quebec, Canada. For more information about Auriesville, phone 518-853-3033.

SIR WILLIAM JOHNSON_____

"He Who Does Much Business"

Called "Warraghyagey" by his Mohawk Indian compatriots, Sir William Johnson certainly lived up to the Indian meaning of his name, "He Who Does Much Business." As the most trusted friend of the Mohawk tribe for four decades, he rose to the position of Superintendent of Indian Affairs in 1756 and was largely responsible for guiding the tribe's destiny through both peace and war.

Johnson came to America to oversee the vast land holdings of his English uncle, Sir Peter Warren. Johnson himself would use his lucrative fur-trading profits to become one of the wealthiest and largest landowners in New York State. At one time, he personally held title to over three hundred square *miles* of fertile farming land along the Mohawk River Valley. The inhabitants of the region, including a large number of Indians, became his tenants and his subjects.

Johnson was no ordinary land baron. He was deeply committed to the nurturing of the land and to the well-being of his people. He became particularly friendly with, and trusted by, the Mohawks. He joined them in battle against the French in the French and Indian War of 1754. He vigorously educated himself on the customs and rituals of their forefathers and earned their respect as a spokesman for their causes. He took on a concubine, Molly Brant, who was the sister of the powerful Mohawk war chief, Joseph Brant. He sired a large number of descendants whose extended families would make up a large segment of his loyal constituents.

Sir William was the most influential figure in Indian affairs in the mid-1700s. So strong was his impact on the life of the Mohawk Nation that even after his death he was revered as a leader, and his policies were adhered to as if he were still alive. Johnson died on July 11, 1774, and was buried in the community that he designed and planned, which was named after him.

Johnstown is located about sixty miles west of Albany, New York, and just five miles north of the New York State Thruway. Johnson is buried on the grounds of St. John's Episcopal Church in the downtown business district of the city, at the corner of Buffalo and Cayuga Streets. This is a bustling hub in the shopping and office center of the city and an unusual place to find a final resting place. The Johnson gravesite is not located in a traditional cemetery. The site is a special spot well within the view of the passing public. A bench and beautiful landscaping make his grave an inviting place. The church itself is a historic and beautiful sight and is worth a visit inside.

A man of some ego, Johnson would probably not argue with the inscription on his headstone:

GRAVE OF SIR WILLIAM JOHNSON, BARONET
1715-1774
(His Indian Name)
"WARRAGHYAGEY"
"He Who Does Much Business"
Founder of Johnstown
Supt. Of Indian Affairs

Major General in British Army
"Colonel of the Six Nations"
BUILDER OF A NATION!

Author's note: Sir William Johnson's restored baronial estate, Johnson Hall, is a centerpiece to any Johnstown historic tour. Many events and exhibits revolve around this home and Johnson's life, and it is a much-visited site. For information, call 518-762-8712. Also of note, if you turn directly around from viewing Johnson's grave, you will look across the busy thoroughfare and notice what is today a Fleet Bank building. There, you will find a brass plaque announcing that this was the birthplace of the founder of the women's rights movement in America, Elizabeth Cady Stanton.

Brig. Gen. Peter Gansevoort____

"Hero of Fort Stanwix"

Of all of the glorious and illustrious forts that have defended freedom down through the history of America, Fort Stanwix holds a unique and special place for patriots. But first, the story of the fort's savior must be told.

In 1778, Peter Gansevoort was commissioned as commander of the ragtag forces at Fort Stanwix in Upstate New York. This valuable outpost was the last military bastion standing in defense of New York's capital, Albany. The fort was an original military installation guarding and controlling the ancient trading routes from the Hudson River to the Great Lakes (a five-hundred-year-old portage known as the "Oneida Carrying Place"). The British were closing in on Albany and had planned a pincer-like battle scenario that called for the convergence of two sizable forces, under the commands of St. Leger and Burgoyne. St. Leger, a brilliant and cunning senior officer, led a force of over two thousand troops (half were Indians) and was aided with the strategic alliance of

Col. John Johnson and Mohawk Indian Chief Joseph Brant. The only thing standing between them and Albany was the dilapidated and undermanned Fort Stanwix, under the command of twenty-eight-year-old Peter Gansevoort.

The officer ordered the fort rebuilt and renamed Fort Schuyler. He waged an aggressive campaign to bolster his five-hundred-man garrison in the face of overwhelming enemy numbers, and eventually added another 250 soldiers to his contingent. Still, the 1,700 well-equipped and highly trained professional soldiers marching on his location seemed to spell certain disaster. With Fort Schuyler well within attack distance, St. Leger sent a white-flag party to the fort to call for the patriots' surrender. Gansevoort rejected the demands and gained precious time.

In a decisive stroke of underhanded genius, Gansevoort had concocted a plan with ally Benedict Arnold (who was moving up the Hudson River Valley with an army to relieve the fort, albeit an army still several weeks away). Arnold released a captive British soldier named Han Yost, who escaped. Yost, a dimwitted and excitable sort, was re-captured by the British. He then regaled St. Leger with tales of a "mighty army" coming to the fort's rescue. So exaggerated was Yost's information (purposefully planted as such by Arnold) that St. Leger called off his siege on Fort Schuyler and ordered his forces to flee ahead of certain death or capture. The scare tactic worked so well that many of the enemy forces retreated in such haste that they abandoned their loaded weapons, artillery, and food stores, all of which Gansevoort put to good use.

Legend has it that at the moment the bombardment of his fort commenced, Gansevoort ordered his men to run a flag up the fort's pole. The banner was made of red packing material, white ammunition shirts, and shreds of British blue uniforms. Although probably an apocryphal campfire story handed down through the ranks of soldiers over the years, a plaque still can be found at the site declaring Fort Schuyler as the place of the "first flying of the Stars and Bars in battle."

After the war, Gansevoort returned to his native Albany and took over the successful business interests of his prominent family. An astute investor, he took great interest in the new region of Saratoga County, then being formed north of Albany, and went and confiscated thousands of acres of land from the former loyalists. He started a mill town there, where the village of Gansevoort, New York, now stands. He died in Albany just shy of his sixty-third birthday in July 1812.

Gansevoort's brother, Leonard, was a delegate to the Continental Congress of 1787-1788. His cousin, Leonard, was the first judge in Albany County. And his grandson, Guert Gansevoort, distinguished himself as a naval officer. He retired after forty-five years of naval service at the rank of commodore.

Author's note: Brig. Gen. Peter Gansevoort is buried in Albany Rural Cemetery, Menands, New York (518-463-7017). The cemetery is located approximately two miles north of Albany. It is one of the oldest and most heralded cemeteries in Upstate New York and counts scholars, soldiers, millionaires, and presidents among its buried (see also President Chester Arthur in this book). Famed Fort Stanwix (Fort Schuyler) is located in Rome, New York. It is a member of the National Parks System and has been called one of the finest examples of fort restoration in America. There are many programs for all ages, particularly in the summer months, when thousands visit. Colorfully dressed interpreters wander the confines of the fort eager to explain and describe the daily life of the American soldier at the time of the siege. The fort is open from April 1 to December 31, from 9 AM to 5 PM. For group tour information, phone 315-336-2090. Battle re-enactments are regularly scheduled, and a fifteen-minute film in the fort's theater gives a detailed explanation of the fort's history. A new million-dollar visitors center has just recently opened.

EXTERMINATOR

"Horse Racing's Legendary 'Old Bones'"

Willis Sharpe Kilmer was a raconteur, a colorful bon vivant, and an extravagant renaissance man. He made huge sums of money in publishing (*The Binghamton (NY) Press*) and medicine (he created and sold the most popular home remedy medicinal product of its day called, believe it or not, "Swamp Root"), was a major real-estate investor in the growing turn-of-the-century Southern Tier of New York, and also owned one of the premier racehorse stables in the state. One of his horses, Exterminator, is among racing's winningest steeds. And his story rivals any in horseracing lore, including the well-told tale of Man O'War. But, it is only by a quirk of fate that we even know of this horse at all!

Kilmer's marquee horse was Sun Briar. The horse was groomed to be a Kentucky Derby contender and was the pride of the stable (which Kilmer named Sun Briar Court). The only problem was that Sun Briar ran erratically during workouts. To remedy this, Kilmer paid $17,000 to the W.G. Knight Farm in Kentucky for a workout partner named Exterminator. The horse had never run a race before but was an excellent companion to Sun Briar and nudged him along to increasing workout speeds. As Sun Briar performed more spectacularly with each training run, Exterminator stayed right with him hoof to hoof. Kilmer proclaimed Sun Briar his entry in the forty-fourth running of the Kentucky Derby for 1918 and bragged to the world that he had a sure-fire winner. Disaster struck when, just weeks before the big race, Sun Briar was injured during a training session and had to be scratched. Still holding a slot in the Derby, Kilmer was convinced (against his better wishes) to enter Exterminator.

On the day of the race, Kilmer's horse, a complete unknown and the longest of long shots (30-1 odds), swept the field and won the crown. A sentimental crowd favorite, Exterminator went on to win fully half of all the races he entered. He ran one hundred races, won fifty, and came in the money eighty-four times. While running his one hundredth race, he pulled up lame and was sent to pasture.

Exterminator, or "Old Bones" as the fans called him because of his lanky and haggard look, was a gentle old soul of a horse who hated to be alone. Kilmer found this out when his trainer realized that the horse wouldn't eat if Sun Briar or another stable-mate wasn't around. Kilmer remedied this problem by buying a small Shetland pony and penning him up with the huge champion. The pony was named "Peanuts." The two were inseparable. They slept in the same stable together, appeared at parties at Kilmer's estate together, and romped in the countryside together. Exterminator's final public appearance came just months before his death when he made a publicity "run" around Belmont Race Track to raise money for the war effort. His final parade down the familiar final stretch that he had seen so many times before was met by a standing ovation by the large crowd in attendance to say goodbye. His faithful sidekick Peanuts was at his side the whole way. His appearance helped raise $25,000,000 in War Bonds that day.

"Old Bones" died in 1945 at age thirty. He is buried in Binghamton, New York.

Author's note: Whispering Pines Pet Cemetery is located just past the Ross Park Zoo, not far from the old site of Kilmer's extravagant estate, which was on Riverside Drive. Cross the Susquehanna River downtown and follow signs to the zoo, or just follow Cross Street to Park Avenue to Morgan, which becomes Gardner Road. The cemetery is just a mile and a half past the front entrance to the zoo. There are several small pet gravestones here, but the one for Exterminator is large and impressive. It carries a life-size profile of the famous horse's head on the front side. Buried in the same plot is Sun Briar (d. 1943), with Peanuts, presumably, somewhere nearby. Exterminator was inducted into the Racing Hall of Fame in 1957.

Other animals of note buried in New York are:

Ruffian (d. 1975) is buried at Belmont Race Track, Elmont

Fala (FDR's dog) is buried at the Roosevelt Home, Hyde Park

Go For Wand (d. 1990) is buried at Saratoga Race Track, Saratoga

Spectacular Bid (1979 Kentucky Derby & Preakness) is buried at Milfer Farms, Unadilla

Little Texas (Teddy Roosevelt rode him up San Juan Hill) is buried at Oyster Bay

And last but not least ... Samantha the Snake (world's largest snake; a twenty-five-foot anaconda) is buried (read "stuffed") at the American Museum of Natural History in New York City.

(Also, Checkers, the famous cocker spaniel pet of the Nixon family and the subject of the turning-point speech in the former president's political career, had been buried at Bide-A-Wee Cemetery in Wantagh, Long Island for decades, but only recently has been reburied at the Nixon Library and Museum in Yorba Linda, California.)

GEORGE CRUM

"Indian Inventor of the Potato Chip"

As Ripley would say, "Believe it or not." George Crum, an Upstate New York American Indian, was the inventor of the potato chip!

Crum, a chef at a classy Adirondack Mountain lodge in Saratoga, New York, called Cary Moon's Lake Lodge, was a crusty, curmudgeonly half-Indian character known far and wide for his talents in the kitchen. The Moon Lodge, on the shores of beautiful Saratoga Lake, was a popular spot with the well-heeled of the day who would flee the stuffy confines of New York by train to hobnob with fellow millionaires and celebrities in the cool Adirondack summer. One of those bluebloods was none other than Commodore Cornelius Vanderbilt, then one of the richest men in America.

On August 24, 1853, as the story goes, "The Commodore" was dining at the swanky hotel when he voiced displeasure at the thickness of the potato wedges he and his companions were served. He told the waiter to tell the chef to cut the potatoes thinner. This went back and forth for several minutes between the millionaire and the Indian chef, until Crum finally decided that he would give Vanderbilt his comeuppance. Crum sliced a half-dozen potatoes so thin you could almost see through them, deep fried them, and sent them out on a plate. Vanderbilt, to the chef's surprise, laughed heartily at the gesture and ate the potatoes with gusto. Soon other diners demanded the "potato crunches" and a legend was born. Crum called his new item "Saratoga Chips," and word of their popularity soon spread (by train, no doubt) to the salons and parlors of New York City, as the millionaires took the story of "Indian George's chips" home with them. One struggles to imagine the conversation in the fancy parlor cars of the private trains of the Vanderbilts, Astors, and Goulds on their return trips downstate. Great titans of finance all discussing the thrilling discovery of a thinly cut, lightly salted fried potato!

On the heels of his new fame and notoriety, Crum, a descendant of Huron warriors and a former trapper and Adirondack Mountain guide, opened up his own lakeside hotel, Crum's House, in Saratoga. The restaurant featured complimentary baskets of "Saratoga Chips" on each table. Crum had five wives, and they, and much of his extended family, made up the core of his employees at this popular restaurant. The fame of "Saratoga Chips" spread nationally when they were included in one of the best-selling cookbooks of the day, *Buckeye Cookery and Practiced Housekeeping*, by Estelle Woods Wilcox.

Crum died on July 22, 1914, at the age of eighty-six and is buried in Malta Ridge, New York.

And so, like Clarence Crane and his Life Savers, Frederick Rueckheim and his Cracker Jacks, and Henry Perky and his Shredded Wheat, here is to you, George Crum, for giving us one of life's little pleasures ... the *potato chip*!

Author's note: Finding the grave of the inventor of the potato chip was one of the most challenging projects of this book. Having begun my research in the 1980s, long before the Internet, George Crum's final resting place took a lot of good ol' detective work. It took me walks through several Saratoga region cemeteries (St. Peter's, Greenridge, etc.) to realize I was coming up empty-handed.

The key to finding his grave was in a long-lost story regarding his last name. Some had told me that George Crum hated the comic overtones of his last name and had it changed for legal reasons to George *Speck* when he was a young man, although he would use Crum professionally. Now looking for a Speck instead of a Crum (!), my task became easier. I found that a George Speck had been born in Malta, New York, in 1828 and discerned that this was my man.

I traveled to the beautiful tiny town of Malta (just twenty miles north of Albany) and did an afternoon of "graveyard snooping." A couple of quick walking trips came up empty. And then, as it had happened dozens of times during the research for *Great Graves*, one man came to my rescue. His name was Mike Peters and he was a Malta cemetery historian. "Sure," he said. "I know just where old George is buried." He dug out the yellowed pages of a Malta history book from a huge oak desk in his living room and flipped right to the cemeteries. Then even *he* became stumped. A quick phone call to a friend confirmed his suspicion. George Speck (Crum) was buried up the road apiece, in even tinier Malta Ridge, New York, in a small rural cemetery. He dug out the grave charts, pored over them with a strong magnifying glass, and then exclaimed, "There! There he is!" I said goodbye to this kindly gent and his wife and headed the four miles up the road to Malta Ridge.

Sure enough, as per Mike's clear directions, I found the old cemetery with no problem. I entered with my hand-drawn map clutched confidently, and there it was, a small, weathered stone that read "George Speck. Born Malta 1828. Died July 22, 1914, age 86."

The exact location of his grave as written on the back of a shopping list by good old Mike Peters is "Malta Ridge Cemetery, Malta Ridge, N.Y. Lot #79, 7 burial plots north of the driveway." The town is ten miles south of Saratoga, and there is an exit to Malta from I-87 (the Northway). Make your first left-hand turn at the first red light and this puts you on the road to Malta Ridge. An ancient little cemetery, there are four Revolutionary War veterans buried here. One curious note: George Crum/Speck's gravestone notes his age at death as eighty-six. Mike Peters' old cemetery journals had his age at death as ninety-six!

ELMER E. ELLSWORTH

"1ˢᵗ Union Casualty of the Civil War"

How many of us can actually say that we ended up doing exactly what we originally wanted to do as a child? How many office workers out there really wanted to be an astronaut? How many secretaries wanted to be a ballerina? Well, Elmer Ephraim Ellsworth *always* only wanted to be one thing ... a soldier!

He dreamed of being a soldier as a young child, and he was determined to never waver from that path. Upon his high school graduation, he applied for the military academy at West Point. He was rejected. His family could not afford to send the young Ellsworth to a private military academy, so he drifted off to Chicago, where he began to study law. His fascination with all things military continued unabated during this time, and he was especially fascinated with a French military organization called the Zouaves. He studied their unique and intricate training methods and even learned the French language so he could better translate the original French Zouave manuals. He eventually attached himself to a group of "weekend soldiers," which was on the verge of disbanding. At last able to put his extensive military expertise to work, Ellsworth organized the disheveled group into a precision brigade that became highly respected for its tight discipline and professional abilities.

He named his new group the "U.S. Zouave Cadets" and exhibited their skills at public shows. Thousands would turn out to see the spectacle of colorfully uniformed soldiers performing their precision marches and their intricate drills. The unit became a major attraction in the Chicago area, and Ellsworth was persuaded to take his soldiers on a nationwide tour. The popularity of the group grew so widespread that he was named Assistant General of the Illinois National Guard, and his Zouaves were named to the prestigious position of "Governor's Guards."

In 1860, Ellsworth joined the law office of Abraham Lincoln and worked tirelessly for his election to the presidency. He personally accompanied Lincoln to his inauguration in Washington. He urged his friend, now president, to oversee a complete restructuring of the U.S. military in preparation for the anticipated hostilities ahead. Lincoln, completely charmed by this young New Yorker, agreed to all his recommendations. So close were the president and the young soldier at this point that Ellsworth had rare access to all sections of the White House, would dine with the president frequently, and became the favorite playmate to Lincoln's young sons. Mary Todd Lincoln considered him "family."

At the very dawning of the Civil War, Ellsworth was sent over the Potomac at Washington to evict Confederate supporters in nearby Alexandria, Virginia. Not a shot was fired as the Union soldiers entered the town. Colonel Ellsworth spied a Confederate flag flying from the top of the city's largest hotel and personally went to the roof to take it down. While coming down the stairs, he was shot and killed by the hotel's proprietor. The Confederate flag was still tucked into his jacket. Doctors could not save the young soldier, and he died on the spot. An onlooker noticed the large medallion around the dead soldier's neck. It read, "NON SUL NOBIS SED PRO PATRIO" ("Not For Ourselves, But For Our Country").

Col. Elmer Ephraim Ellsworth became the first Union casualty of the Civil War.

Upon being told of Ellsworth's death, Lincoln collapsed at his desk and sobbed uncontrollably. "I cannot talk. Ellsworth is dead and it has unnerved me greatly." The president ordered a state funeral of unprecedented grandeur for Ellsworth. His funeral was held right in the White House, where hundreds passed his casket to grieve. His body was then moved to New York City, where it lay in state for three days as more than five thousand came to mourn. Ellsworth's body was then placed on a funeral boat and sent to Troy, New York. There a specially commissioned "mourning train" was dispatched to take the young soldier's body to his hometown of Mechanicville, New York. He was finally buried with full military honors in that town's Hudson View Cemetery. Because of the extensive mourning period for Ellsworth, many experts believe that he was the first person in the U.S. ever to be embalmed.

A direct reaction to Ellsworth's death was a surge of recruits joining the Union army. The popular patriotic phrase of the day was, "Remember Ellsworth," and one large New York military unit was named "Ellsworth's Avengers."

At the time of his death, Ellsworth had just turned twenty-four.

Author's note: Hudson View Cemetery is located off South Street, high on a hill in the southern area of Mechanicville, New York, eighteen miles north of Albany. Markers will guide you to his gravesite. His grave monument is one of the most impressive this author has ever seen, a towering monument topped by an eagle with his wings spread wide. It is unmistakable. An inscription on the grave reads, "I am confident that he who knoweth even the fall of the sparrow will have purpose even in the fate of one like me." The grave is tended by the local historical organizations in Mechanicville and is usually resplendent with flowers and patriotic adornments.

JENNIE GROSSINGER

"The Catskill's Innkeeper"

When I first met Frank Kubiak, his face was a road map of wrinkles and his hands showed the roughness of a person who has never shied away from work. He was retired, well into his seventies, and living with his longtime wife in a cottage in the hills overlooking Worcester, New York. Frank had worked for many years at Grossinger's Resort in the Catskills, "back in the good old days." His time served as a kitchen helper at the famed resort in the 1930s is still vivid in his mind. "It was a real family affair then," he recalled in his thick Eastern European accent. "Harry (Jennie's brother) was the real brains of the outfit. He did the books and the buying for the whole place himself. The mother (Malke) was very tough. I remember once when she came into the kitchen and discovered a milk pot being used for a meat dish. Well, since Grossinger's was a strictly kosher place back then, the mother flew into a rage. Malke grabbed the pot right out of my hands and dumped the contents on the floor. She then lugged that big pot all the way down cellar where she took an ax and smashed it to bits! But Jennie," remembered the elder Kubiak with a twinkle in his eyes, "Jennie was the charmer of the bunch. She knew us all by name and treated us with fairness and kindness. She showed real affection for her help. I will never forget her."

Such were the feelings of many for famed Catskill hotel owner Jennie Grossinger. In 1914, she and her husband (a third cousin also named Grossinger) moved into a dilapidated seven-room country house near Liberty, New York. Strapped for income, she rented the rooms out during their first summer there and netted a grand total of $81 for her efforts! Later she would add on, buy up surrounding farms and homes, and eventually build her rooming business into a hotel. Tourists fled the steamy summer confines of New York City for the cool mountain setting of her country resort, and soon she was able to accommodate more than five hundred guests at a time!

Jennie Grossinger's secret weapon was her genuine friendliness. An attractive, elegant hostess, she remembered all of her guests' first names and treated each visitor as if she or he were a celebrity. And many were! During the hotel's halcyon days, one would not be surprised to scan the main dining hall and see the likes of Bobby Kennedy, Jonas Salk, Frank Sinatra, Eleanor Roosevelt, and her two favorite Rockys: New York Governor Nelson Rockefeller and boxing champ Rocky Marciano. Rocky (the boxer) even wore a satin robe into the ring for his fights with the hotel's name emblazoned across the back. Singer Eddie Fisher sang there as a struggling, unknown entertainer. So fond of the place (and Jennie) was Fisher that he later returned to Grossinger's and married Debbie Reynolds on the grounds.

The memories of Grossinger's are of a time of laughter and fun in the historic "Borscht Belt" of Upstate New York. By 1972, the resort was taking in over 7 million dollars a year and boasted its own ski lodge, lake, airport, and post office. A few years in the early 1950s, however, were difficult ones for the famed hotel when two devastating fires brought death and destruction to the idyllic grounds of the resort.

The most serious fire, on March 1, 1954, killed eight employees while injuring nearly thirty more. Still, the glamour and the reputation of this famed Catskill Mountain icon would not die, and the landmark resort was fully restored through commitment and hard work, and remained one of the many success stories of this rural vacationland.

Jennie Grossinger lived a happy and fulfilled life surrounded by family and friends to the end. When she died on November 20, 1972, at the age of eighty of a massive stroke, she could truly have claimed to have been loved by all who met her. She remained loyal to her hotel even after her daily responsibilities were diminished by her age. She died at "Jay Cottage," a home that was built for her directly on the hotel grounds so she could always be near "her place."

She is buried in Ahavath Israel Cemetery in Liberty, New York. Just a short distance south from Grossinger's, on NYS Route 52, make a left on the gravel road with markings to the cemetery. Just three hundred feet up this road you will see the first unmarked entrance to Ahavath Israel on your right. Enter here and immediately on your left, on the rise of a small knoll, you will see the large granite stone reading GROSSINGER. Jennie is buried here with her entire family.

Author's note: The decades of the 1980s and 1990s saw the ultimate demise and slow death of the "Borscht Belt" as it had been known for many years, and Grossinger's went broke. Cheap airfares, second vacation homes, nearby entertainment meccas like Atlantic City, and ever-present air-conditioning all but made the need to escape the summers in New York City to the aging Catskill resorts a thing of the past. Huge, lumbering hotels, once filled with the smells of Jewish cooking and the sounds of "dirty dancing" are mere ghosts of an era long past. Businesses and homes are more for sale than not. It is truly one of the most depressed areas of New York State. But, like the basket in which all of the proverbial eggs are placed, legalized gambling is beginning to look like the lone savior to this Phoenix waiting to rise. New York has all but authorized Indian-reservation gambling in the region, and stirrings of activity are everywhere. In 1999, Grossinger's was purchased for six million dollars by a consortium that promises to restore the grand resort to its five-star reputation of the past. As for Jennie, both a hospital and a nursing home in Israel still bear her name in tribute to her many generous acts to Jewish charities and other causes.

EMILY POST

"Etiquette is the science of living."
"There is no reason why you should be bored when you can be otherwise."

With those simple credos, Emily Post established herself as the "Paragon of Politeness" and the arbiter of social rules in America for over fifty years. She always believed that manners and etiquette were something to be taught and learned rather than bred or assumed. Her first book on etiquette was published in 1922 and instructed the reader (in simple terms) on acceptable behavior required to become socially decorous. Her theories on such timeworn dilemmas as "which fork to use" or "when a hostess is served her meal" were dealt with in a concise and sensible manner. Her reading public loved it, and, at the time of Ms. Post's death in 1960, *Etiquette in Society, in Business, in Politics and at Home* (Funk and Wagnalls) was nearing its 100th printing!

Her style of writing was flowery and depictive, yet homey to a fault. For example, in her first book, she describes proper behavior at a funeral this way: "The last place in the world you would look for comfort at such a time (a funeral) is in the seeming artificiality of etiquette. Yet it is in this moment of deepest sorrow that etiquette performs its most vital and real service." She then goes on to describe how etiquette "draws the shades, muffles the bells, keeps the house quiet, and hushes the voices" in a house of mourning.

She wrote in this style through chapter after chapter of problematic social crossroads. Chapter titles included "Cards and Visitors," "The Clothes of a Gentleman," "House Parties at Camp," "Teas and Afternoon Parties," "One's Position in the Community," and "Salutations of Courtesy." It sold in the millions.

While not exactly born with a "silver spoon in her mouth," Emily was brought up in a comfortable lifestyle in Baltimore, Maryland. She would eventually go to private schools and attend an exclusive girls' finishing academy. In 1892, she married banker Edwin Post and had two sons, Bruce and Edwin, Jr. The marriage ended in divorce, and Mr. Post later died in a boating accident. Despite the breakup, she called herself Mrs. Price Post for the rest of her life (Price was her family name).

A prolific writer, Post was the author of many books. Some were related to her field of etiquette, while others were written just to satisfy her penchant for prose. In fact, her novel *The Tile Market* was a bestseller. But etiquette paid the bills and generated a huge fortune for her over many years. Over two hundred newspapers carried her daily advice column, which she wrote right up to the time of her death. Her peak readership was 7,000,000 a day. She hosted a popular radio show and wrote the best-selling *Emily Post Cookbook*.

Emily Post never retired. She believed in the refinement of the social graces in every area of daily life and wrote tirelessly on behalf of the benefits of knowing what was proper and what was not in sundry social predicaments. Shortly before she died, she penned a series of newspaper articles on driving manners. She was appalled at the social disarray evident on America's burgeoning highways, and she set about to lay down a code of etiquette to be used by all drivers.

She died on September 25, 1960, at the age of eighty-six. She is buried in her longtime hometown of Tuxedo Park, New York.

Author's note: St. Mary's Cemetery at Tuxedo Park is located just inside the imposing gated stone walls of this private community. Tuxedo Park is located about an hour's drive north of New York City. Exit the New York State Thruway (I-87) at 15A (Sloatsburg) and follow Route 17 four miles to the town. The guard at the gated wall will let you in to go to the cemetery. It is located right behind the church, and the stone bearing the name MRS. PRICE POST is easily found among the few gravesites here.

The Emily Post Institute, founded by Emily herself in 1946, continues to thrive under third-generation Posts. Her great-grandchildren Peggy, Peter, and Cindy oversee an etiquette empire that includes seminars, magazine columns, books, and more. It is located at 444 South Union Street, Burlington, Vermont. Their mother, Elizabeth Post, was the direct successor to Emily. Granddaughter Elizabeth Post revived and updated *Emily Post's Etiquette* five times from 1965 to her retirement from the institute in 1992. Great-granddaughter-in-law Peggy Post reissued the book (the seventeenth edition) in 2004. It ranked #5 on the Amazon.com list of bestsellers for that year!

Tuxedo Park is an exclusive cloister of wealthy New Yorkers. Founded in 1886 by tobacco millionaire Pierre Lorillard, five thousand acres were acquired through shrewd business investments and (some say) winning poker hands! The community was constructed by nearly two thousand Italian stonemasons in less than one year. The finished town had its own racetrack, clubhouse, spa, police station, stores, and thirty miles of roads. It was known as the place where the "New York 400 came to play." The mansions of the rich and famous of the turn of the century housed a Blue Book-full of blue-nosed multimillionaires. Legend has it that Lorillard introduced the short-waisted coat worn by Prince Albert in England to the States. First worn by Griswold Lorillard at the Autumn Ball, the high point of Tuxedo's society year, it was quickly named the tuxedo and became a popular alternative to the more rigid white tie and long tails worn by the elite of the day.

SAMUEL J. TILDEN

"I Still Trust the People!"

For a man who was a winner most of his life, Tilden is probably most remembered for the election he *lost*! And it was a big one, the presidency of the United States. And he lost by a single vote. And there were no hanging chads to blame.

Tilden was born on February 9, 1814, in New York and would become one of the state's most prominent "political lions." In 1867, as chairman of the New York State Democratic Party, he took on the notorious "Tweed Ring" in New York City and its onerous leader William "Boss" Tweed. Many thought that Tilden had embarked on a classic mission of political suicide. Tweed had virtually every city official and office-holder in his well-lined pockets, and his nefarious influence was felt at every level of state government. Tilden was tenacious in his attacks on Tweed, and, through deft legislative maneuverings and a "crusade-like" devotion to the dethroning of the corrupt leader, he was triumphant in reforming the face of New York City politics forever.

A former New York State assemblyman, he was elected governor in 1875. A respected and influential leader of his party's reform movement, Tilden's popularity grew immensely during his term in office, and at the Democratic National Convention in St. Louis on July 27, 1876, he was nominated to be the party's national standard-bearer. His Republican opponent was to be another governor, Rutherford B. Hayes of Ohio.

The Hayes-Tilden election of 1876 is still being studied today. One of the bitterest in memory, the contest was fiercely fought from one end of the country to the other. On the morning after the election, all signs pointed to a Tilden victory. He held a 184-165 margin over Hayes in the electoral count and was winning the popular vote by a quarter-million votes. Still, the electoral votes in Florida(!), Louisiana, and South Carolina (and a single vote in Oregon) were seen as unofficial and could sway the victory to the Republicans. Teams of supporters from both sides streamed into the contested states to "shore up" their candidate's votes. Threats, bribes, payoffs, scandals, and the intimidation of party hacks (thugs) were all employed to influence the electors' votes. It was American politics at its worst.

Finally, a commission was empowered to settle the dispute. The commission was to be equally divided between the parties, but at the last moment, a Hayes supporter was appointed to the swing seat. In a vote strictly along party lines, the commission decided 8-7 in favor of declaring Governor Hayes the winner of *all* the disputed electors, thereby giving the Republicans the White House. Tilden continued to hold a 250,000-vote lead in the popular vote, even after the election was officially declared over.

Ignoring pleas to run again in 1880 and 1884, Tilden retired from public life and spent the final years of his life amassing a huge fortune from his business interests. He died on August 4, 1886, and with no immediate family to leave his money to (he was a lifelong bachelor), he bequeathed much of his six-million-dollar fortune to the State of New York for the establishment of the New York Public Library.

New Lebanon, New York, is located ten miles west of the Massachusetts border and thirty miles east of Albany on NYS Route 20. It is a sleepy, bucolic town in the heart of the Shaker region of Eastern New York. The Cemetery of the Evergreens is the largest cemetery in the village and is located near the junction of NYS Route 22 and Cemetery Road, just north of the community. Enter the main gates of the cemetery and proceed just a short distance and you will notice the elaborate Tilden tomb. It is located in the center of a large, well-manicured, round plot that is separated from the other graves in the cemetery. With its grand marble lion heads and intricate funereal carvings, it is certainly one of the most impressive final resting places this writer has ever seen. Chiseled across the front of the large tomb are the words, "I STILL TRUST THE PEOPLE!"

Author's note: New Lebanon is truly in the heart of the Shaker region. It would be well advised for the visitor to take in any of the several Shaker sites during an afternoon visit to this beautiful region of New York. From Tilden's grave, you will be only minutes from the well-known Shaker Village at Hancock, Massachusetts, and the Shaker Museum at Old Chatham, New York. Of course, New Lebanon itself was the original home to the United Society of Believers in Christ's Second Appearing (Shakers), and their museum always has interesting events and exhibits going on. The New Lebanon Shaker Village passed into private hands when the last living Shakers moved from here in 1947. The massive stone walls and foundations of the buildings—all that remain from a devastating 1972 fire that gutted the commune—are a sight to behold, measuring up to fifty feet wide, two hundred feet long, and as high as four stories tall. Visitors come from all over to view this architectural marvel. The New Lebanon Shaker Village is one of only six places in the U.S. listed on the Top 100 list of endangered historic places by the World Monuments Watch List of Endangered Sites. They can be reached at 518-794-9500.

EDNA ST. VINCENT MILLAY

"Pulitzer Prize"

During the 1930s, Edna St. Vincent Millay was called the "foremost woman poet in America."

In 1917, she published her first volume of poetry, *Renascence and Other Poems*, to much critical acclaim. In fact, *Renascence*, a beautiful depiction of nature's poetic glory, would remain one of her most famous works. She moved to New York's Greenwich Village, where she commiserated with other "free spirits" of the burgeoning American poetry culture and immersed herself in the wild living offered in New York's "Little Bohemia." Her poems began to reflect her newfound freedom. She wrote famously of "burning the candle at both ends" and of having no regrets at doing so.

Her 1923 release, *The Harp Weaver and Other Poems*, was hailed by the critics as a masterpiece, and she won the Pulitzer Prize for poetry for it. Millay was the first American woman to win this award.

She spent the last thirty years of her life in the quiet, rural setting of her mansion, "Steepletop," in tiny Austerlitz, New York. She died of a heart attack in 1950 and is buried deep in the woods at her home.

Author's note: Finding Edna St. Vincent Millay's grave was a daunting task. Having arrived at Steepletop on a glorious autumn day, I found it busy with hikers and walkers attending the artists' colony there. A dirt road bisects the property between her home and her farm. I came upon some joggers. When asked, they pointed me to a walking path that disappeared into the woods about a half-mile up from the farm. After trekking through the beautiful woods nearly a mile, I came upon her gravesite. A large rock with a plaque bearing the names of Edna and her husband marks her grave, which is surrounded by an old, ornate, black wrought-iron fence. With no markings on the road to this spot, the visitor is best advised to wait for one of the colony's artists or employees to happen by and ask. It is worth the effort. The forest, especially in its full autumnal bliss, is magnificent. If you listen, you can hear the hum of the automobiles up ahead and over the next hill on the New York State Thruway crossing the Massachusetts line. Austerlitz lies snug against the border of the two states, just southeast of Albany. Steepletop, now a recognized National Historic Landmark, has been fully restored and is a privately owned writers' colony established in 1974 in Edna's name by her sister. Since then, more than one thousand artists have come to these spectacularly peaceful seven hundred mountaintop acres to hone their skills at composing, artistry, visual arts, and writing. Steepletop is located at 444 East Hill Road just outside of town. Austerlitz, population 1,500, was named by Martin Van Buren after he found that residents in Seneca County had named a community after Napoleon's greatest defeat, Waterloo. Austerlitz, of course, was the scene of Napoleon's greatest victory.

Of interest to Millay fans is the famous Whitehall Inn in Camden, Maine. Here she wrote *Renascence* and first recited her poem of seeing three hills and three islands and the beauty of the surroundings there. The nineteen-year-old's first audience consisted of a few hotel guests and employees. The inn, recently celebrating its centennial year, is a magnificent old New England landmark known for its service, beauty, and comfort. In the main building, it displays a multimedia exhibit on their most famous guest. Phone 207-236-3391 for information and reservations.

GERTRUDE BERG

"Yoo Hoo, Mrs. Bloom!"

"Yoo hoo, Mrs. Bloom" was the television battle cry signaling an evening of laughter in the 1940s and 1950s. The cry would echo across a brick Brooklyn tenement courtyard from the unpainted sill of an open window. The window's only adornment was a flower struggling for life sprouting from an old rusted Sanka coffee can. The large woman leaning far out into the slit of sunlight was the one and only Gertrude Berg, in the persona of one of America's most beloved television characters, Molly Goldberg.

First on radio and then on television (and then movies and *then* Broadway), Molly was the very personification of Jewish motherhood. Sort of an *I Remember Mama*—Yiddish style! Her essayer, Berg, was an enormous talent who was equally blessed as both a writer and an actress. Her forty-year show-business career was marked with brilliant creativity and a high degree of professional excellence, both in the spotlight and out.

Berg was born on October 3, 1899, in Jewish Harlem in New York City but soon moved to the Catskill Mountains to work in her family's resort. Inspired by the wisdom and humor of her own immigrant family, she began submitting scripts to radio. After several initial disappointments, she hit the big time with her affectionate look at an extended family (much like her own) living in a crowded apartment in New York. She called it *The Rise of the Goldbergs*, and it quickly became a national sensation. From the mythical Mrs. Bloom, the object of her opening line bellow, to her husband, Jake, and their two teenage children, Rosalie and Sammy, the entire Goldberg clan and their hilarious Tremont Avenue neighbors became the second most popular comedy show on radio (just behind *Amos and Andy*). In fact, from its opening night show, November 20, 1929, Gertrude Berg would become Molly for several generations of fans. Sure she tweaked it, refined the character, grew with the scenario, and expanded the cast (much like Lucille Ball did with her successful reinventions of her Lucy character), but she always kept the core of Molly sacred: wise, funny, inquisitive, loving, and strong.

Later renamed *The Molly Goldberg Show*, it won every major entertainment award there was, and she warmly invited unknown talents on to hone their craft. Anne Bancroft, Van Johnson, John Garfield, and Joseph Cotton were all newcomers on her show. When she took the franchise to television in 1949, she bagged one of the most lucrative contracts in the business. Recognizing that she was the writer, creator, *and* star of the show, she was a power to be reckoned with (again, much like Lucy). Her steady legion of 15,000,000 loyal radio fans easily made the transfer to her TV show, and she was one of the medium's earliest and biggest successes. Berg won an Emmy Award in 1950 for Best Actress in a television comedy.

While she never completely divorced herself from her Molly character, one could hardly blame her for not trying. She appeared as Molly on radio for nearly two decades, was on television for several years, wrote a bestselling *Molly Goldberg Cookbook*, starred in the autobiographical *Me and Molly* on Broadway for 156 performances in 1948, and got the full-blown Hollywood treatment in the big picture *Molly!* in 1951. America, it seemed, could never quite get enough of "Yoo hoo, Mrs. Bloom!" and Molly laughed with her audiences all the way to the bank.

In the late 1950s, Berg turned her exuberant talents toward Broadway and away from Molly for the first time. In what she called one of the highlights of her professional life, she starred as a widowed Jewish mother (Mrs. Jacoby) opposite the erudite Sir Cedrick Hardewicke's wealthy Japanese widower in the acclaimed *A Majority of One*. All right, so the role *was* that of a Jewish mama. Still, Berg amazed critics with the depth of her acting talent and her ability to stay scene for scene with an accomplished British thespian. At the age of sixty, she was all of a sudden the hottest thing on Broadway, and she walked away with the Tony Award for Best Actress for her part. She returned to Broadway in 1963 and was cheered for her critically praised performance in *Dear Me, the Sky is Falling*.

In the autumn of 1966, she was rehearsing yet another play for New York, this one based on her own script, when she felt ill. On September 10, 1966, she went to a doctor's appointment and was admitted into a hospital for routine tests. She died of a massive heart attack four days later. She was sixty-six.

Gertrude Berg is buried in Fleischmanns, New York.

Author's note: Clovesville Cemetery is one of the smallest of all that I have visited. Coming north into town on Route 28 (Delaware County), take your second exit into the village (Depot Street) and cross the bridge. Make a left and the cemetery is less than a mile down the road on your right. Enter the cemetery and proceed to the gated Jewish section in the rear (Congregation B'nai Israel). There are a small number of grave markers here. On the highest knoll in the western section of this part of Clovesville, you will see the Berg family plot.

Captain
William Van Schaick_____

"Vindicated!"

One of the most tragic and forgotten disasters in American history is the fire aboard the steamboat *General Slocum*. This tragedy claimed more lives than any other American disaster until the terrorists struck the World Trade Center on September 11, 2001. And yet few have ever heard of it.

On June 14, 1904, more than 1,300 parishioners of St. Mark's Lutheran Church, a German landmark on Sixth Street in New York's Lower East Side, gathered along the shores of the East River to board the *General Slocum*, a 350-foot-long paddle-wheel steamboat, for an afternoon outing to Locust Point, Long Island. The church had chartered the 265-ton boat for $350. Most of those going on the outing were mothers and their school-age children celebrating the end of the Sunday school year.

The throng filled every inch of the boat, from stem to stern. Oom-pah bands played German favorites, and families, all in their proper Sunday best, laughed and visited with friends and neighbors. The sky was blue and the weather was perfect.

As the boat headed north up the East River, near 90th Street, the first sign of trouble appeared. Smoke began billowing up from a corridor, where apparently a fire had started. The people began inching away from the smoky area and waited for the crew to extinguish the fire. They waited and waited as the fire grew and grew. The captain of the ship, William Van Schaick, was not notified for a full eight minutes. By then, the blaze was out of control, and panic had gripped the *Slocum*.

With shooting orange flames chewing their way along the decks, people began donning the more than three thousand life preservers. Tragically, the flotation devices had long lost their usefulness, and the buoyant cork inside them had disintegrated into dust. Those who had strapped on the lifesavers soon sank to the bottom of the river, weighed down by their layered finery. Fire hoses were unrolled and manned by the men and crew. The hoses, having never been used, burst upon the first pulse of water and were useless, having rotted with age. The lifeboats were fastened to the ship and could not be used. The passengers were doomed.

The *Slocum*, completely ablaze and shrouded in smoke, could be seen clearly by the bystanders along the shore. These onlookers screamed for the ship to dock on the west shore of the river, the nearest point. Captain Van Schaick, however, realizing the potential for a greater disaster should the shoreline oil storage tanks meet up with the flaming ship, proceeded up river a mile, to North Brother Island, through the treacherous currents of Hell's Gate. By the time he landed, the ship was a charred ruin, strewn with bodies and listing badly. The death toll would eventually reach an astounding 1,021. The captain survived.

The *General Slocum* had passed an inspection just a month before the tragedy, and questions needed to be answered. And blame needed to be assigned. Captain Van Schaick became a lightning rod for the anger and grief of the thousands of family members looking for a scapegoat to punish. The captain and officials of the Knickerbocker Steamship Company, the parent organization, went on public trial. Captain Van Schaick was the only person convicted. He was found guilty of criminal negligence and manslaughter. He was sentenced to ten years in prison and was delivered to Sing Sing Prison in Upstate New York.

Van Schaick had a long career as a trusted sea captain and always felt that he had done his best to avert tragedy that fateful day. He truly believed that by making his decision to bypass the shoreline and to try to make North Brother Island he was acting to save as many lives as he could. An inquest was formed to study the case and later decided that it was the steamboat company and their lack of inspection guidelines that had led to the deaths of more than one thousand innocents that day. Van Schaick was vindicated after serving nearly half of his term. He was pardoned by President William Howard Taft and released from prison.

Captain William Van Schaick spent the final years of his life in desolation and anonymity. He died in 1927 and was buried in an unmarked grave at Oakwood Cemetery in Troy, New York.

Author's note: Many people are familiar with the Triangle Shirtwaist Fire of 1911, seven years after the *Slocum* fire. In that tragedy, 146 young immigrant girls died because greedy business owners had locked the doors of their high-rise sweatshop, thereby sealing their fate when a fire broke out. Much speculation is offered as to why this fire, terrible as it was, is more imbedded in our memory than the more calamitous *Slocum* fire. One school of thought has it that the German victims of the boat fire grew less and less sympathetic as World War I approached in Europe. Others feel that the Irish girls who leapt to their deaths in the factory fire were much more heartbreaking in that their deaths were caused by a direct act of greed by their bosses. As one *Slocum* survivor said, "The Triangle girls were overworked and oppressed. We were just on a family picnic." In any case, two great similarities grew from the dual disasters. Both spawned major overhauls in safety regulations for their respective fields. The factory fire brought on sweeping changes in workplace safety rules. The *Slocum* fire ushered in an age of stricter safety regulations in the steamship business.

An amazing effect of the *General Slocum* fire was the change it brought in the German neighborhood of the Lower East Side. Once a thriving, productive community of 80,000 nationals, within one census period, the German population in that area was almost totally wiped out. Hundreds of funerals, buildings draped in black bunting, lines of dozens of hearses, and whole schools emptied of their young students had all but erased any fond memories for the surviving German families, and most moved out of this sad area to leave it to the next wave of immigrants.

In 1999, a grandniece of Captain William Van Schaick erected a monument over his grave in Oakwood Cemetery. It reads, "Captain William Van Schaick, 1837-1927. VINDICATED!"

A year after the *Slocum* fire, a large memorial was unveiled to the victims buried in the Lutheran Cemetery at Middle Village, Queens, New York. Sixty-one unidentified bodies were interred in a single mass grave there. Little Adele Liebenow, just an infant in 1904 and the youngest survivor of the ship fire, had the honor of ceremoniously pulling the flag off the monument revealing it to the large crowd assembled, which included many other survivors and their family members. On January 26, 2004, Adele Liebenow (now called Adella Wotherspoon) died at the age of one hundred. She was the last living passenger from that terrible day in 1904, having gone from the youngest survivor to the oldest.

Each year on June 15, a memorial service is held at the cemetery monument to honor the memory of those aboard the *General Slocum*.

Oakwood Cemetery is located off Oakwood Avenue in Troy, New York. "Uncle Sam" Wilson and Russell Sage, also in this book, are interred here as well. Van Schaick's grave can be found in the center of Section S1. Maps of the cemetery are available at the front office.

LEVI P. MORTON

"Servant of a Nation"

Few official positions in the U.S. government are subject to such scorn and ridicule as that of vice president. Being largely a ceremonial role, the vice presidency has swallowed up more dedicated public servants than almost any other position. A sage public observer, John Nance Garner (a one-time Veep), once called the job "akin to a bucket of warm spit." The roll call of number-two men in the White House is a litany of forgotten names obscured by time and the job itself. The names of Schuyler Colfax, George Mifflen Dallas, Charles Fairbanks, and Thomas Hendricks scarcely register a glimmer of recognition when spoken of today. Probably the name Levi Parsons Morton is equally unknown. But most of these men, in their pre-vice-presidency days, were men of great political stature who had carved out respectable, if limited, public service careers. None, however, could match the impressive resume of Levi Morton.

Born in Vermont in 1824, he early on established a personal and public life in neighboring New York State. Working in the wholesale goods business, he built up and headed Morton & Grinnell Company, one of the largest firms of its kind in the East. Morton rode through the mid-1860s on a wave of prosperity and good fortune until he suffered an almost fatal business setback. In 1861, his business went broke because of forfeiture of Southern debts to his company at the start of the Civil War. He reorganized his firm after the war (1869) and eventually regained his reputation, stature, *and* fortune. He was a wise and flinty financier who became a leader in the American banking industry. Due to his vast expertise in national and international business, it wasn't long before the major political parties came calling looking for a candidate.

Morton's first foray into politics ended in defeat, when as the Republican nominee for the 45th Congress in 1876, he was defeated. He re-established his political base and won two years later and then won again in 1880. President James A. Garfield then named Morton to be his U.S. Minister to France, where he served for five years. In 1889, he went to Washington, D.C., as Benjamin Harrison's vice president.

A strict rule enforcer, Morton adhered to the tightest dictates of Senate procedures when he was called upon to officiate over that body. One story tells of Morton forgoing lunch breaks so as to prevent the Senate from "acting out of sorts" in his absence.

After leaving the White House, Morton returned to the Hudson Valley and ran for governor. He won and spearheaded civil-service reform as the major goal of his administration. He retired from public office in 1897 at the age of seventy-three but would enjoy a fruitful life for many years to come. He reorganized his substantial financial holdings, created the Morton Trust Company, traveled extensively, and enjoyed the lively companionship of his many friends. He entertained lavishly and regularly at his palatial estate in Rhinebeck, "Ellerslie," and it was here at his home that he died on May 16, 1920, his ninety-sixth birthday.

Morton is buried in Rhinebeck Cemetery.

Author's note: Morton's final resting place features a large, verdigris-covered monument including a list of all of the important positions he held during his long public service career. The epitaph across the top of this list reads, "Servant of a Nation." Enter the main gate of the cemetery (off Route 9) and proceed to the rear and southern edge of the cemetery to find it.

Morton had five daughters and held many festive parties for them at Ellerslie over the years. Little is left of the original mansion, and it is privately owned. Its grounds, which once needed fourteen gardeners to tend it, are still intact. Morton was the wealthiest and most famous resident of Rhinebeck, a quaint village on the east side of the Hudson River just two hours north of New York City. He employed many of the residents of Rhinebeck in his businesses and at his many interests, homes, and farms. At the age of eighty-five, he sold his Morton Company to J.P. Morgan, who then changed its name to the now-familiar Morgan Guaranty Trust. One of the most interesting facts regarding Morton's life is that, as Minister of France, he actually accompanied the Statue of Liberty to New York Harbor where it was erected. The statue was shipped in many large pieces all at once.

There are two "must-sees" to take in during your visit to picturesque and historic Rhinebeck. One is Cole Palen's Olde Rhinebeck Aerodome (845-752-3200), the oldest original "living" museum of antique aircraft in America. Maybe you will be lucky and witness the flying of (under perfect weather conditions *only*) their 1909 Bierot plane, the oldest flying aircraft in the country. Also, The Beekman Arms Hotel on Main Street is a wonderful step back into history. Presidents from George Washington to Franklin Roosevelt have stayed here, the oldest hotel in America (845-876-7077).

GRACE BROWN

"An American Tragedy"

Young Grace Brown was a beautiful country girl working in a drab garment factory in Cortland, New York. The boss's nephew, Chester Gillette, was smitten with the diminutive lass, known to all of her friends as "Billy," and pursued her with tenderness and sincerity. They took long, lingering walks together, sharing their dreams of the future. In a short time, however, Chester started to feel the constraints of emotional entanglement and tried to end their relationship. Grace would have none of that and begged him to stay with her. Chester relented, the romance continued (although the passion had rescinded for him), and they went on seeing each other, living in the same town and in fact working at the same factory. Their lives would change dramatically in the spring of 1906 when Grace announced that she was pregnant.

Chester wanted out of the relationship immediately and plotted the grisly denouement of their love affair. On the guise of taking a vacation, the couple left by train for an outing in the remote

Adirondack Mountain lake region of far northern New York State. There, on Thursday, July 11, 1906, they rented a rowboat and left their hotel (The Hotel Glenmore, Big Moose) for a row around the lake. By nightfall, Grace Brown was dead and Chester Gillette had vanished.

On the following day, a search party discovered the drowned girl's body, and within a few days, Gillette was caught and arrested for her murder. Such was the beginning of the most celebrated murder case of the early twentieth century.

Hundreds of onlookers stood in the rain to see the murder suspect arrive at the local jail (Herkimer, New York) in handcuffs. Tours were added at the lock-up to afford the public a view of the suspect's cell. New York City newspapers sent reporters upstate to cover the scandalous story. Rumors were fanned and embellished. And through it all, Chester Gillette stoically proclaimed his innocence.

Passions ran deep against the accused murderer. Headlines screamed his every move, and spectators scorned his lack of remorse. *The New York Morning Telegraph* sent its most famous reporter, Bat Masterson, to cover the trial. Courtroom drama went unchecked. In one high point, the prosecutor brought to court a cloth-covered bottle containing, he said, the fetus taken from Grace's body to prove her pregnancy. He never revealed it.

To the surprise of no one, Gillette was found guilty of murder and sentenced to death in the electric chair. His mother, Louise, waged a highly emotional (and highly publicized) clemency campaign to no avail. Gillette was electrocuted at Auburn State Prison on March 30, 1908. His body is buried in an unmarked grave.

Grace Brown's murder remained news for years. In 1926, Theodore Dreiser wrote his now-classic novel, *An American Tragedy*, about the case, and it was a huge bestseller. His fictionalized account of the murder featured "Clyde Griffiths" in place of the real Chester Gillette and Roberta "Bobbie" Alden in place of the real Grace "Billy" Brown. In 1931, Paramount Pictures produced a film based on Dreiser's account of the crime, starring Sylvia Sydney in the role of Roberta/Grace. In 1951, the movie was remade as *A Place in the Sun*, with the victim's role now being played by Shelley Winters. The 1951 movie was one of the year's biggest hits, and it rekindled serious interest in the Adirondack murder.

Tiny South Otselic, New York, is located about twenty miles west of Norwich in upstate Chenango County. As you enter the town from the south (on NYS Route 26), you will see Valley View Cemetery on your right, on a hill across from the Fire House. Make a right on Gorge Avenue and travel past the footbridge. The cemetery entrance is on your right. Halfway down the main entrance road, on your right, you will see a small gravestone reading, "Grace Brown. At Rest."

Author's note: A trip to Herkimer, New York, will reveal many interesting facets of this famous trial. The Red Brick Court House, where the trial actually took place, still stands, an 1870s-era architectural beauty. Across the street is the Old Herkimer County Jail where Gillette was held during his incarceration. His cell was on the third floor. The basement today holds a museum with many period artifacts including a complete trial transcript. You will also find papers and artifacts concerning the "other great murder case" in Herkimer County's past. The trial of Roxalana Druse is remembered here in all its grisly details. She was convicted of murdering her husband, chopping his body into small chunks, and burning them in the kitchen stove! If you go around behind the jail, you can still see the boarded-up wooden door she exited the jail from to step out onto the hanging platform. Above the door you will see the hook from which the hangman's noose was strung. She was the first and only woman ever hung in the county. The Herkimer County Historical Society, at 400 North Main Street, can provide you with much information about the Gillette and Druse trials, which elicited great national interest nearly a century ago and still draw many visitors to this rural county seat. In fact, the society even holds re-enactments of the trials from time to time! They can be reached at 315-866-6413.

ERNIE DAVIS

"Pride of the Orangemen"

Ernie Davis's potential was so great, his star so bright, that an NFL football team retired his playing jersey *before* he ever played a single professional football game. His story, so sad and yet so inspirational, is one of the greatest sports stories of them all.

An incredible natural athlete, Ernie Davis came thundering out of the sandlots of Elmira, New York, and shot his way to the top almost instantly. A multi-record holder in high school, "The Elmira Express" was courted by virtually every major college in the East upon his high school graduation (and before!). Disciplined by a strong-willed mother (he said he never remembered his father, who died in a car accident when Ernie was a child), he finally took her advice and agreed to the offer placed in front of him by Syracuse University. His mother liked the idea of him being at a school close to home and family, and the college's offer was substantial, but not unlike that of several others. The deciding moment came when a dramatic visit took place at Ernie's Elmira home. SU had dispatched his hero, Jim Brown, to "get the kid signed." Davis enrolled in 1958 and played his first varsity game as an Orangeman in 1959.

A veritable engine of a man, his tenacity and sure-footedness enabled him to set school records in several areas, all in his *first year on the squad!* Some of those records stood for years; some still stand today. His total yards gained (3,414), points scored (220), average per-play yardage (6.8), and total number of touchdowns (35) even surpassed the records that had stood during Jim Brown's tenure as SU's superstar.

The six-foot-two, 225-pound powerhouse was a popular student on campus and was described as gentle and courteous by his classmates. Because he was black, and a campus celebrity, a certain amount of inherent racial backlash was expected, and he carried his mantle with dignity. As a student, he achieved only modest success in his grades, but he became the most popular ambassador for the sprawling Northeastern university.

Davis's glory days on the field at Syracuse were filled with many memorable highlights. Perhaps the two most dramatic moments were the 1960 victory over the University of Texas at the Cotton Bowl (where Davis, ignoring racial slurs from fans, scored two touchdowns and was voted the game's MVP) and the Liberty Bowl game of 1961 (against Miami). In this game, with SU down by three points at halftime, Davis energized his team with a spectacular 140 yards rushing total and carried his team to victory.

In 1961, he entered the history books forever when he was named the first African-American Heisman Trophy winner. The award, given annually to the nation's best collegiate football player, was the high point of Davis's career.

After his SU graduation, every major team worth its wallet (even Canadian football teams!) offered the new graduate the moon. He chose to follow his heart once more (and his hero) and signed with Jim Brown's Cleveland Browns for $80,000 per year. As the top draft choice in the nation, the world of sports was clearly his oyster.

In July of 1963, while practicing for an exhibition game against the Green Bay Packers, Davis fell ill with what he thought was mononucleosis. He was ordered to bed by the team physician for a short recuperation. Setback after setback kept him in the hospital for months as the doctors tried desperately to pinpoint his ailment. Finally, left with no other choice, Cleveland placed him on the disabled list for what would have been his first professional season. He would never don a football uniform again.

With his family and himself never really understanding the severity of his illness (leukemia), Davis kept the hope of a football career alive for months. But, after weeks of deteriorating health, he passed away quietly in his sleep on May 18, 1963, at Lakeside Hospital in Cleveland. He was twenty-three.

The sports world, thinking he had been recovering, was in shock. Ernie's SU coach, Ben Schwartzwalder, who had called him "the perfect athlete and the perfect gentleman," postponed all practice at SU in Davis's honor. Art Modell, the president of the Cleveland Browns, flew to Elmira to console Davis's mother. The entire city of Elmira declared an official three-day period of mourning. The funeral itself was the largest ever held in Elmira and drew the national spotlight to this Southern Tier community. His body lay in state at Neighborhood House, a community center where he had played sports as a child. Thousands of citizens passed by his open casket to pay their last respects. Pallbearers were members of his old high school football team. Honorary pallbearers included the *entire* twenty-six-member roster of the Cleveland Browns. Jim Brown, the hero that Ernie Davis never got to play alongside of, led the delegation. Twenty-five thousand mourners jammed the funeral service at the church, where a message was read from President John F. Kennedy calling him "a young man of great character and inspiration." Davis's mother collapsed and was carried from the service. An eighty-car procession carried the young superstar the mile and a half to Woodlawn Cemetery, where he was buried the next day.

His small gravestone can be found in the Evergreen East section, near the center of the cemetery, just above Babyland.

Author's note: Woodlawn Cemetery also is the final resting place of Samuel Clemens/Mark Twain (also in this book). The cemetery is located at 1200 Walnut Street at the corner of Walnut and West Hill Street. Syracuse University struggled for years with ideas of how to properly honor "Legendary #44." When the famed Carrier Dome was built to house the university's sports center, the college chose to host a permanent memorial there. On the first level of the Dome, behind the home goal posts, you will find the Ernie Davis Room. Here for all to view is the story of the most famous Orangeman of them all. Designed in dark, muted tones, the room holds a revolving display of university sports events and artifacts. At the entrance, behind a reverently lit display case, is the famous Heisman Trophy won by Davis in 1961. Next to it is a giant photograph of Ernie Davis in action on the playing field. There is no admission charge to this room, which is open when a home sporting event is underway. SU retired jersey #44 in his honor (the Cleveland Browns retired his #45 for the same reason, before he had ever played a down for the team). The Syracuse University Carrier Dome is itself a marvel to behold. Seating 51,000 people, it is the fifth-largest domed stadium in the U.S. For information about the Dome and the Ernie Davis Room, phone 315-443-4634. The football legend is also remembered each year when the National Leukemia Foundation gives its annual Ernie Davis Award to a "football player, past or present, who exemplifies Davis's qualities of excellence of character and integrity and service to mankind." Elmira remembers its favorite son in many ways. One of the most impressive is a $100,000 larger-than-life bronze statue of him erected on June 19, 1988, in front of Ernie Davis Middle School, which he attended when it was Elmira Free Academy. The plaque reads, "ERNIE DAVIS: A football player ... a student ... a friend ... a hero. He lived life with integrity, and died with courage."

VAN BUREN, FILLMORE, ROOSEVELT, AND ARTHUR

"Four U.S. Presidents"

Except for the state of Virginia (with its Arlington National Cemetery), New York is the final resting place of more American presidents than any other state. All of us were numbed by years of factual overkill about our presidents while we were in school (e.g., James Buchanan was the only bachelor president; Lincoln was born in a log cabin; Taft installed a special bathtub because of his large size; Truman loved to walk; Ike was a golfer; Kennedy needed a rocking chair; Johnson was a rancher; etc.), so to continue the numbing process in this book seems pointless.

Since this book is focused on the *Upstate* New York final resting places of the famous, we will not explore the *downstate* graves of President U. S. Grant (New York City) or President Theodore Roosevelt (Young's Burial Ground, just east of Glen Cove, Long Island). As for the other four, well, there *are* some interesting facts about these presidents who "reside forever" in the Empire State that are fun to know. For example, did you know FDR is buried with his pets? Or that President Fillmore is buried in a plot with *both* his wives? And even the places they ended up being buried at speak volumes. Two are buried in towns they were born in (Franklin D. Roosevelt and Van Buren). And two are among the most visited tourist sites of their kind in New York (Grant's Tomb and FDR's Hyde Park). Except for Millard Fillmore, all of the former presidents buried in New York are within just a few miles of the Hudson River.

Let's take a look at the burial places of the eighth, thirteenth, twenty-first, and thirty-second presidents.

MARTIN VAN BUREN was born on December 5, 1782, becoming the first U.S. president to be born *after* the signing of the Declaration of Independence. He was a lifelong resident of Kinderhook, New York, and began his political career there. He occupied almost every major position in the U.S. government during a career that spanned a half-century. He was elected New York State Senator (1812), New York State Attorney General (1816), United

States Senator (1821 and 1827), Governor of New York (1828), U.S. Secretary of State (1829), Vice President (under Andrew Jackson), and, finally, President. His career at the highest levels of government came at a crucial time for our nation, a period of expansion and growth as well as a time of great turmoil and tumult. His life was long and fruitful. He was born during the Revolutionary War, and he died during the Civil War. Although diminutive in stature (he stood barely five foot six), Van Buren cut a wide swath through the halls of power both in New York and in Washington, D.C.

President Van Buren is buried in Old Kinderhook Cemetery, Route 9H (Albany Avenue), just outside of town. His grave is a mere mile from the place he was born.

Author's note: Surprisingly, no great attention is given to the fact that a former U.S. president is buried in this small, rural cemetery. Save for the ubiquitous New York State blue and yellow historical marker, you would never know the prominence of the cemetery's most famous inhabitant. Van Buren's tall obelisk is the most imposing monument here, however, and his grave is very easy to find.

Van Buren purchased his magnificent Kinderhook estate, Lindenwald, in 1839, and today it is a National Historic Site. Few visitors come to this stately Hudson Valley mansion, however, perhaps choosing instead to travel down the road a few miles to the more popular Hyde Park, New York, home of Franklin Roosevelt. Because of this, the lack of visitors is a welcome relief compared to the tour buses and school groups that throng to FDR's home. Lindenwald is comprised of a large family home, complete with bell tower, and 226 acres of fertile Hudson Valley farmland. It is located at 1013 Old Post Road, Kinderhook, New York, and you can call 518-758-9689 for tour information. It is open to the public from May through October, seven days a week. One of the highlights of the tour is the original intact wallpaper that was hand-painted by the former president himself! It is said that John Van Buren, the president's son, lost the family home in a card game. The "winner" of Lindenwald was the Jerome family. Their daughter, Jennie Jerome, became Prime Minister Winston Churchill's mother! Van Buren was such a fixture in Kinderhook politics and society that his well-known nickname was "Old Kinderhook." His supporters would call out to him at rallies and gatherings by his initials, and some believe that is the root of the saying "OK" (meaning everything is good). On December 9, 1943, the U.S. Navy commissioned the Ashland Class Dock Landing Ship the *USNS Lindenwald*. It received five battle stars during World War II.

MILLARD FILLMORE was a towering political figure in western New York State. Born in Locke, New York (Cayuga County), at the dawning of the new century (January 7, 1800), he moved to Buffalo in his twenties and would be connected to the city for the rest of his life. He represented the city in Congress twice (1833 and 1837) and was elected comptroller of the state in 1847. Elected as Zachary Taylor's vice president,

Fillmore ascended to the presidency upon Taylor's death on July 9, 1850. After he left the White House, he returned to his beloved Buffalo, where he was a pillar of society, an influential power broker, and a generous contributor to the well-being of the city. He served as the first chancellor of the University of Buffalo, was a founder of the Buffalo Historical Society, founded Buffalo General Hospital (now Millard Fillmore Hospital), and was a deep-pockets contributor to many local charities. Upon his death, he was remembered as a great friend to the city and its residents. He is buried in the family plot at Forest Lawn Cemetery, 1411 Delaware Avenue (at Delavan Street). Just a small bronze plaque identifies the grave as that of a former U.S. president.

Author's note: Forest Lawn Cemetery is filled with outstanding architecture and historic funereal sculptures. The cemetery was built in 1849, covers 269 acres, and has about 170,000 residents. Many of Buffalo's elite are interred here, including William Fargo (of Wells and Fargo), Seneca Chief Red Jacket, and others. Fillmore's family plot contains many members of his family, including *both* his first and second wives (the first Mrs. Fillmore, Abigail, caught a cold while attending the inauguration of her husband's successor, Franklin Pierce, and died twenty-five days later). A larger-than-life statue of Fillmore, by world-renowned sculptor Bryant Baker, graces Buffalo's City Hall Plaza. Its inscription sums up the love and respect the city had for its most famous citizen: "Millard Fillmore. Lawyer. Educator. Philanthropist. Statesman." Note that like the lack of markings at his gravesite, the statue also respects his modest nature and mentions only his contributions to the city rather than to the nation as president. Fillmore's home in East Aurora, New York, just outside of Buffalo, is a National Historic Landmark. He and Abigail lived there from 1826 to 1830, and the house contains many of his personal artifacts. It is open to the public Wednesday, Saturday, and Sunday, from 2 to 4 PM. It is located at 24 Shearer Avenue in this tiny community. A curious factoid is that Buffalo actually gave our country *two* presidents. Grover Cleveland was brought up in Buffalo and served as the city's mayor before going on to the White House. He too is recognized with a great statue in the downtown business area (Cleveland is not, however, buried here). Millard Fillmore Hospital made international news in 1963 when the very first heart pacemaker was implanted in a patient there.

CHESTER A. ARTHUR the *man* was much more inspiring than Arthur the *president*.

He was the second vice president to become chief executive upon the assassination of the president. (Andrew Johnson followed the murdered Lincoln.) When President Garfield was shot in the back while waiting for a train in Washington, D.C., Arthur was immediately whisked to the capital. Garfield hovered between life and death for more than ten weeks, while Arthur quietly insinuated himself into the Oval Office. When Garfield finally succumbed to his wounds, Arthur became the first president to sit in the Oval Office without ever being elected to office before, except to the vice presidency. (Of course, Gerald Ford would perfect this maneuver nearly a century later when he would become vice president and then president without ever being elected to either position!)

Arthur was a steady, if uninspiring, steward, and what his administration lacked in innovation it made up for in integrity and moral leadership. Arthur was not re-nominated for a second term in his own right, and retired from public life in 1894.

Chester Arthur's public and private personas were as different as day and night. Perhaps a bit haughty or even regal in his public stature, in private he was a gregarious, charming socialite who loved ballroom dancing, female companionship, and natty attire. He owned more than eighty suits! He was an avid outdoorsman and was passionate about fishing. After breaking free of the constraints of a decades-old political life, Arthur would have preferred to have had a much longer retirement than he actually had. He died on November 18, 1896, just eighteen months after leaving the White House. He was just fifty-six.

Author's note: Arthur was predeceased by his wife and is buried with her in Albany Rural Cemetery, Menands, New York. Going north from the city of Albany on Route 377, the cemetery is located at the end, where the road stops. Another entrance can be found off Broadway, just under the I-787 underpass. His enormous black marble sarcophagus (Section 24) is lorded over by a towering guardian angel, and is one of the most striking gravesites in a cemetery filled with impressive memorials. The cemetery is a sprawling five-hundred-acre park-like place. Manicured lawns, beautiful fountains, flowering trees, and interesting graves dating to the Revolutionary War all make this cemetery worthy of a day-long visit. Knots of young joggers and picnicking families enjoy the bucolic setting as if it were a public park rather than a cemetery. The main office will gladly give you a pre-printed map of the area so you may wander the stone paths and even peer out over the edge of the cemetery boundary and view the Hudson River. Dozens of famous names are found at Albany Rural Cemetery (all denoted on the hand-out map at the office), including Brigadier General Peter Gansevoort (see his entry in this book); fifty-five mayors of Albany including Erastus Corning (the longest-serving big city mayor, 1942-1983, in U.S. history); former New

York governor John Taylor (it was in his home that the words that led up to the deadly duel between Hamilton and Burr were spoken); Stephen Van Rensselear, who took the first train in U.S. history, and then later founded Rensselear Polytechnic Institute; Major Philip Schuyler, "The Hero of Saratoga"; and two Americans whose faces appeared on U.S. currency, former U.S. Secretary of State William Marcy and former U.S. Secretary of Treasury Daniel Manning. For cemetery hours and information, call 518-467-7017. Albany Rural Cemetery is located on Cemetery Road, Menands, New York.

FRANKLIN DELANO ROOSEVELT is judged by experts to be among the top three greatest U.S. presidents in poll after poll (along with Washington and Lincoln). Someone once said that "more words have been written about FDR than have been written about all of the other presidents combined." I will not try to add more words to this legacy, but some observations about his life, death, home, and final resting place seem appropriate. Roosevelt's home, gravesite, and library are the most visited of any former U.S. president (although Ronald Reagan's is now attracting large crowds). Vast displays of FDR memorabilia, guided tours, prize-winning gardens, miles of footpaths, inspiring Hudson River vistas, and entertaining public events all make the Roosevelt home and library a busy locale. FDR was born here (his crib is still on display), lived here, and is buried here, but he did not die here. Franklin Roosevelt died in Warm Springs, Georgia, at the "Little White House," his summer home. He was sitting for a watercolor portrait by famed artist Elizabeth Shoumatoff when he was struck with a massive cerebral hemorrhage. (His last words were either "Just fifteen minutes more, please," or "I have a terrible headache," according to various reports.) The beloved president's death stunned the world, which was still at war. ABC-RADIO first reported the president's death by breaking into the children's program *Captain Midnight*, at 5:47 PM on April 12, 1945, with what has been called the briefest wire bulletin in history: "FDR DEAD." The funeral train up the East Coast to Hyde Park was compelling in its grief and grandeur, perhaps rivaled only by the outpouring of sentiment following the murders of John and Robert Kennedy.

Franklin and Eleanor Roosevelt are buried in the rose garden at Springwood, the official name of his home. The day this tight-knit community said goodbye to its favorite son was a somber one for all. FDR had visited Hyde Park more than two hundred times during his administration and was re-charged and re-energized after each visit. (In late 1944, with the war grinding on and in failing health, he told a confidant, "All that is within me cries out to go back to my Hudson River home.") The mansion, purchased by Roosevelt's father in 1867, is one of the most splendid of all the Hudson River estates and receives thousands of visitors each year. It is located on Route 9 just south of the village of Hyde Park. Springwood was named a National Historic Landmark shortly after the president's death, on November 21, 1945. It has restrooms, handicap accessibility, water fountains, food concessions, and a well-stocked gift shop. One must plan on at least one full day to see all that FDR's home has to offer. The museum is jam-packed with thousands of FDR-related items, including his 1936 Ford Phaeton automobile with the custom hand controls that allowed him to drive. Eleanor's home, Val-Kill Cottage, is also close by ("The only home I have ever owned," she wrote). It is the only National Landmark dedicated solely to a first lady, named as such on May 26, 1977. Tours of Val-Kill run in conjunction with those at Hyde Park. When visiting the Roosevelt graves, notice the small white marble tablets scattered in front of their giant tomb. On these tablets are the names of the family pets that have died through the years, including the most famous "First Dog," Fala. For information regarding tours and events at Hyde Park and Val-Kill, phone 1-800-FDR-VISIT.

Four sons of Upstate New York who rest eternally in the communities that meant so much to them. Three of them buried near the banks of the Hudson River, and one buried within sight of the Great Lakes. Millard Fillmore in Buffalo with just a modest graveside notation of his achievements, Van Buren also with no presidential fussiness in Kinderhook, Arthur in a grand (yet hardly ever visited) tomb in the state's capital city, and Franklin D. Roosevelt at his majestic Hyde Park estate, which is visited by thousands each year.

Johnny Evers

"Tinkers to Evers to Chance"

Immortalized in the now-famous Franklin Adams 1910 poem *Baseball's Sad Lexicon*, the tongue-friendly phrase "Tinkers to Evers to Chance" has been chanted by sandlot ballplayers for decades. But who was Tinker? Evers? And who, by chance, was Chance?

All three were baseball stars for the Chicago Cubs shortly after the turn of the century and were feared as the greatest double-play combination in the sport. Johnny Evers was from Upstate New York, so let's start with him.

Evers (rhymes with beavers) was the important center cog at second base in this historic trio. He joined the Chicago Cubs full-time in 1903 and helped lead the Cubbies to three straight NL pennants. A powerful hitter as well as one of the league's most dominant infielders, Evers batted .350 in *both* the 1907 and 1908 World Series. Nicknamed "The Crab," for his low-crouching fielding style, he was one of the two or three key players for the

Cubs during those years. He also had a part in what has been called the most controversial baseball game ever played.

On September 23, 1908, with the National League pennant at stake, the Chicago Cubs and the New York Giants were locked in a 1-1 tie, men on first and third, bottom of the ninth with the Giants at bat. The hitter drove a hard single to the outfield, easily scoring the player on third to end the game. EXCEPT that in order for the play to be ruled *completed* nineteen-year-old Fred Merkle, making his first start of the year as a pinch-runner on first, had to *touch* second base. When the Giants runner at third crossed home plate, swarms of Giant fans streamed onto the field in jubilation and chaos. In this confusion, Merkle just turned and headed for the outfield clubhouse, considering the game completed and won by his Giants. At this point, Johnny Evers, seeing that Merkle had failed to touch second base, started screaming for the ball, got it, and ran and tagged second base *essentially* putting Merkle out. A riotous confrontation between the teams ensued, and finally the exasperated umpires could not rule one way or another on the strange play so ordered it ruled a tie game and said it must be played over. It was, and the Cubs won the game and took the pennant from the N.Y. Giants. Poor Fred Merkle was never spoken of again in New York, except when fans recalled the "Merkle Boner," as it became known. Evers' knowledge of the rules of the game gave his team the win.

Tinker, Evers, and Chance all ended up managing the Cubs. In fact, Johnny Evers managed both Chicago teams, the White Sox and the Cubs (the only player to do so). While they were forever linked by the singsong sound of their famous triple-play sequence, the three players were hardly close friends off the field. One time a feud erupted in the clubhouse between Chance and Tinker, and it quickly escalated into fisticuffs. They would not speak to each other for more than thirty years after that. Despite the tantrums and grudges, Evers maintained a high level of professionalism once the game began. A fan favorite, he was even saluted with his own day, a rare tribute. May 10, 1913, was "Johnny Evers Day" at the Polo Grounds in New York City. He performed well for the visiting contingent from his Troy, New York, hometown. He slammed a single, a double, and even scored the winning run in the Cubs' victory over the Giants.

Johnny Evers spent his retirement years involved with business and baseball in Albany. He suffered a stroke in 1942. He died of a cerebral hemorrhage in St. Peter's Hospital, Albany, New York, on March 28, 1947, after spending his twilight years in poor health, seated in a wheelchair behind the counter of his Albany, New York, sports store. He was sixty-five. He is buried in St. Mary's Cemetery, Troy, New York.

Frank Chance, the first baseman, was the first to go. Known as "The Peerless Leader," he had a knack for attracting the beanball and eventually had to retire from baseball with head injuries. He suffered brain disease and died very young on September 24, 1924, just a few years after leaving baseball. He is buried in Rosedale Cemetery, Los Angeles, California.

Shortstop Joe Tinker, who once stole home *twice* in a single game, suffered from diabetes most of his life and, after a double leg amputation, died on his sixty-eighth birthday on July 27, 1948. He is buried in Greenwood Cemetery, Orlando, Florida.

All three were inducted into the Baseball Hall of Fame in Cooperstown, New York, in 1946. Evers and Tinker, who hadn't spoken to each other in decades, were moved to tears at the emotion of the moment.

Author's note: St. Mary's Cemetery in Troy is located at 79 Brunswick Road (also known as Route 22). Follow the main road into the cemetery to Section B. Johnny Evers is buried in Lot 237, Grave 3, next to his wife, Helen, who died on January 1, 1974. A towering five-foot statue of Christ atop the nearby Hannan family plot will guide you to Evers' gravesite. For cemetery information, call 518-272-0931.

R.I.P.

JOHN BROWN

*"John Brown's Body Lies
A' Moulderin' In The Grave..."*

John Brown was an unmitigated failure when it came to business. He tried everything, it seemed, and he always failed. From sheep raising to land surveying to tanning animal skins, he was always running from debt. He did set one personal goal in his life, a goal of missionary proportions. The abolition of slavery. And this goal cost him his own life and that of several of his sons.

It was said that Brown's hatred of slavery began when he was just five years old. He witnessed a black slave, just a child himself and a close friend of his, being beaten unmercifully by his master. Brown tried to intercede on his young friend's behalf and received a terrible thrashing of his own. That incident would spark his life's burning passion. He would go on to become the preeminent abolitionist activist of his time.

In the 1840s, wealthy anti-slave organizer Gerrit Smith offered plots of land high in the remote Adirondack region of Upstate New

York to free blacks who wished to settle the land there on farms he purchased. In 1849, Brown, being chased by creditors, settled his family in North Elba (just outside of Lake Placid) on land he purchased from Smith for just $1 per acre. His reputation had clearly preceded him, and soon he was considered a man of great leadership qualities in the all-black community. Author Richard Dana, who met Brown, a white man, during this time, dubbed him "King of the Negroes." From his new remote outpost, Brown began expanding his anti-slavery activities throughout the region and the state, and by the late 1850s, he was openly engaged in the direct confrontation of pro-slavery forces.

He and his many children (he had *twenty* children by two wives) formed a "core army," directing the forced freeing of slaves. Brown's righteous cause met its moment of destiny when the Kansas-Nebraska Act of 1854 was instituted, causing the anti- and pro-slavery forces to engage in open warfare in the new, desolate free territories of the West.

He moved his family to Kansas. They settled in Osawatomie, a tiny farming community, where he organized an abolitionist militia. Referring to himself as "Old Osawatomie Brown," his pitched battles with pro-slave forces were fierce and bloody. In the end, one of Brown's sons was slain, and his Kansas town was burned to the ground.

This deadly turn of events caused a noticeable unbalancing of Brown's demeanor. Many thought the tragic events at Osawatomie had caused Brown to become deranged. In fact, his mother, his first wife, and two of his sons *were* outright insane. His zealous behavior became more and more dangerous and unpredictable.

He tried to raise an "Army of Emancipation" but found blacks, by and large, unwilling to take the risks. Frederick Douglass and Gerrit Smith, both longtime friends and supporters, encouraged his efforts, but many others in the movement thought that more could be gained by peaceful, legislative means. Brown became more daring and more foolhardy, attacking farms and settlements with his small band of marauders, freeing slaves and killing slave-owners. Many innocent people were killed by mistake. Eventually, even the U.S. government considered him a rogue outlaw and put a warrant out for his arrest.

In a final attempt to put some life in his movement, Brown and his small band of men set their sights on a sleepy town just north of Washington, D.C. Here, at Harper's Ferry, West Virginia, the U.S. Army kept a large munitions store, weaponry badly needed by Brown's militia. With a band of thirteen white men and five freed slaves, they assaulted the arsenal and captured it. Delaying their escape for unknown reasons, the Army had plenty of time to surround the captured buildings and wait for a surrender. Brown and his men went out with guns blazing, and when the smoke was cleared at Harper's Ferry, ten raiders and seven U.S. troops were dead. Two of the dead were sons of John Brown. He was arrested and placed in chains and taken to a Charlestown, Virginia, federal prison. After recovering from his serious wounds, he was placed on trial for murder and treason. He was convicted.

Brown was given the death sentence and hanged on December 2, 1859, in front of a large gathering of federal troops. Others were convicted and hung also. John Brown rode to the gallows that day sitting on his own coffin in the back of a hay wagon.

Brown had directed that his body be removed to North Elba for burial. A large entourage of family and friends escorted his remains to the Adirondacks, where he was buried on his farm six days after his death.

Author's note: John Brown's grave and farm are located on John Brown Road, just off Route 73, on the southern outskirts of Lake Placid, New York. A member of the New York Parks Association since 1995 and a National Historic Landmark since 1998, there are many signs to lead you to this much-visited place. In fact, the grave of John Brown, as well as the grave of singer Kate Smith in Lake Placid, is among the most visited places in the immediate area (Smith is also included in this book). Brown's farm has been restored to circa-1860 condition and offers many historical signs and photos. His gravesite, near the farmhouse, consists of boulders and monuments and a large, imposing statue of John Brown with his arm draped around the shoulders of a young African-American boy. In 1999, at the rededication ceremony of the site, New York Parks Commissioner Bernadette Castro spoke of Brown, "The life of John Brown and his commitment to the anti-slavery cause helped shape the history of our nation. It is fitting to memorialize his lifelong commitment to the abolition of slavery, and that of his sons and comrades, in this humble setting that he called home." Amazingly, in attendance that day in 1999 were Mrs. Douglas Sutcliffe, great-grandniece of Aaron Stevens, a Brown supporter who was hanged at Harper's Ferry with Brown, and Mrs. Ann Chetsky, great-grandniece of Oliver Brown, who was killed at the raid. Both are buried at John Brown's farm. Another John Brown site of importance is his home in Guys Mills, Pennsylvania. This restored house is where John Brown lived with his first wife. He was a postmaster of Guys Mills, and the remains of his failed tannery are still evident. Inside the museum at the house are original artifacts from his life, including an actual rifle used at the raid at Harper's Ferry. Brown's first wife and two of his children are buried here in marked graves. Two thousand people a year visit this free museum. It is located at 17620 John Brown Road (off Route 77) in Guys Mills, which is twenty-five miles south of Erie, Pennsylvania. Call 814-967-2099 for tour information. Of course, Harper's Ferry, West Virginia, is one of the most spectacular National Historic Sites in America. It is beautifully restored to its original 1850s era condition, and the story of John Brown's raid is vividly recalled through re-enactments, video presentations, and costumed interpreters.

Virginia O'Hanlon Douglas____

"Yes, Virginia, there is a Santa Claus!"

Eight-year-old Virginia O'Hanlon was disturbed when some of the poor children in her town blamed their bleak Christmas on Santa Claus. They told her that if Santa was real they would have received more presents than they actually did. Later, at home, she asked her father if there really was such a person as Santa Claus. Dr. Philip O'Hanlon, a respected surgeon with the New York City Police Department, advised his young child that, while he believed there was a Santa Claus, she should write to the *New York Sun* newspaper and ask them. "If you see it printed in the *Sun*, then it is so," he told her. From that innocent father-daughter chat emerged one of the most inspiring and enduring pieces of Christmas folk history.

Virginia took pen in hand and poured out her confusing situation in what would become the most famous "Letter to the Editor" ever written.

"Dear Editor: I am 8-years-old. Some of my little friends say there is no Santa Claus. Papa says, 'If you see it in the *Sun*, it is so!' Please tell me the truth. Is there a Santa Claus?" She signed it, "Virginia O'Hanlon, 8 years old, 115 W. 95th Street, New York City, New York."

As fate twists its curious course through history, Virginia's letter landed on the desk of Francis Pharcellus Church. He was one of many editorial writers at the *Sun,* and it was prophetic that the little girl's letter was given to him to answer. A crusty, twenty-year veteran of journalistic battles (and real ones, for he was a former war correspondent), Church seized this opportunity to reveal a softer, more sentimental side to his readers. In a direct and charming manner, belying his dour demeanor, Church recognized the child's heartfelt sincerity and answered in kind.

"Yes, Virginia, there *is* a Santa Claus! He exists as certainly as love and generosity and devotion exist, and you know that they abound and give to your life its highest beauty and joy. Alas! How dreary would be the world if there were no Santa Claus! It would be as dreary as if there were no Virginias! There would be no childlike faith then, no poetry, no romance to make tolerable this existence.

"We should have no enjoyment except in sense and sight. The eternal light with which childhood fills the world would be extinguished." The response was signed, simply, "*The New York Sun*".

The response to this exchange of letters was overwhelming. The *Sun* was deluged with requests for the editorial, and media outlets all over the country wanted to know more about the little girl who started the whole thing. While the commotion over the "Yes, Virginia" letter soon died down, it has remained a holiday fixture ever since. Both the child's letter and the editor's response have been printed and reprinted thousands of times in the holiday seasons since the dawning of the twentieth century. Since it first appeared in 1897, it has been reprinted around the world, also, in more than twenty-five languages!

What became of little Virginia? Well, she left her fame in the light of her youth and pursued a career in education. She remained out of the limelight for the rest of her life—well, for 364 days of each year anyway. But on Christmas Day each year, some intrepid writer was always trying to catch up with her and retell the story of her famous letter to the *Sun*. She became a highly respected educator, receiving her BA from Hunter College in 1910, her master's from Columbia University in 1911, and a doctorate in education from Fordham University in 1935. She spent nearly fifty years teaching in New York City schools before retiring. Her last position was as principal of P.S. 401 in Brooklyn, New York, a school for chronically ill children.

Francis P. Church died in anonymity on April 11, 1906. Because of the *Sun's* policy of NOT signing their editorials or letters to readers, no one knew that it was he who was responsible for the paper's now-legendary reply. Even his own obituary in the *Sun* omitted his contribution to Christmas lore. He died childless.

Virginia O'Hanlon (Douglas) spent her final years living with her daughter, Mrs. Robert Temple, in Upstate New York, just southeast of the Capital District. Even in her autumnal years, people would refer to her as the "Yes, Virginia" lady. She died in a Valatie, New York, nursing home on May 13, 1971, at the age of eighty-one. She is buried in North Chatham.

Author's note: North Chatham is a postcard-perfect little town in Columbia County, less than an hour's drive from Albany. North Chatham Cemetery is located just north of the village at the intersection of Route 203 and Route 32. Virginia's grave is easy to find in this small, rural cemetery. Just enter at the first set of stone pillars and one of the first graves on your right is hers.

While in the Chatham area (and there is a Chatham, an Old Chatham, a Chatham Center, and a North Chatham all within ten miles of each other), be sure to visit the world-famous Shaker Museum and Library. Thousands go there every year to witness the "premier center for the interpretation and exhibition of Shaker life and culture." If you ever wanted to know how the Shakers made those *round boxes* or why they hung their chairs on the walls, well, here is the place to get your answers. Its many barns and buildings hold continually changing displays and the museum has an active list of events each year. The museum is located at 88 Shaker Museum Road in Old Chatham (518-794-9100). For more on the story of the Shakers, read the entry in this book for Mother Ann Lee, the religion's founder, who is buried in the original Shaker Cemetery just outside of Albany. By the way, the only active Shaker community left in America is the Sabbathbay Lake Shaker Village in Gloucester, Maine. Less than a handful of the last, elderly Shakers still live there.

ANN TROW LOHMAN_____

"The Wickedest Woman in New York"

In the 1980s, Leona Helmsley was known as the "Queen of Mean." The press painted her as an egomaniac who fired her help for little or no reason, a cheat who fudged her own tax returns ("Only little people pay taxes"), a seductress who snared the elderly owner of the Empire State Building and married him, and a narcissistic old woman who changed her appearance through computer enhancing. And she did jail time! But it's one thing to be called mean and be the butt of jokes in the media and another thing to be called mean and be vilified by *virtually everyone*! Now that is mean ... and that is Ann Trow Lohman.

Time has been just a little bit kinder to the reputation of Ann Trow Lohman than real life actually was. In the mid-1840s, all of New York was abuzz with the news of this despised woman, called "The Wickedest Woman in New York" by the tabloids of the time.

As a young woman, Lohman married a "quack" doctor and changed her own image to that of a mysterious creature called "Madame

Restill" (an invented name). She was an abortionist by trade. She "treated" many of New York's high-society women for their "problems" and gained fame and influence over the course of a few short years. Madame Restill had many friends in high places and was said to have carried everyone from politicians to police chiefs on her payroll.

Restill's fame grew even wider following several widely publicized skirmishes with women's groups and law enforcement agencies. Although she was arrested many times, her political clout allowed her to escape harsh treatment. One time, however, in March of 1846, following the enactment of stringent new laws that made abortion the equivalent of murder, she was arrested, charged, and convicted. She was sentenced to the infamous Blackwell's Island Prison. A newspaper uncovered the fact that Restill was spending her confinement in comfort and luxury in private quarters at the jail, and a scandal erupted. At the height of the controversy, the warden of the prison was fired, and Restill found herself again front-page news.

Although she grew quite wealthy through her abortion activities, she became a pariah to all. She was so despised and hated by her neighbors that the buildings that adjoined her mansion stood vacant for years for want of a tenant. Ostracized by society, she took considerable delight in riding in her fancy carriage up and down ritzy Fifth Avenue in full view of her shocked detractors.

Her husband died in 1876, and she retired and vowed to walk the straight and narrow. That was not to be the case. With her influence vastly diminished, she was arrested in 1878 on what many believe to be the trumped-up charge of "possession of immoral articles." Everyone knew it was payback time for Restill, and it was obvious that she was the victim of a vendetta by the New York Society for the Suppression of Vice. Perhaps too tired to once again face the harsh, scornful eye of the public and press (or perhaps just to get the last word in), Madame Restill slit her own throat with a large carving knife while taking a bath on the evening of April Fool's Day, 1878. Through suicide, she would finally be left alone. She left an estate valued at close to $1,000,000.

Some say the times were too harsh on Ann Lohman. Some say she performed a necessary service in a time of un-enlightenment regarding women's issues. Others say her reputation was richly deserved.

Lohman/Restill's funeral went unattended and unnoticed by all.

Author's note: "The Wickedest Woman in New York" is buried with her husband in the Hudson Hill section of Sleepy Hollow Cemetery, Sleepy Hollow, New York. Enter the cemetery at the main gate, off Broadway. Veer right onto Camp Grove Avenue, which becomes Ivy and then Lawrence Avenue. On your left is a section of old graves. Her tall Victorian obelisk is in the center. Eerily, her grave monument is topped by the white marble life-sized figure of a sleeping child!

As noted in the other Sleepy Hollow Cemetery listings in this book (William Rockefeller and Andrew Carnegie), this is a much-visited place of beauty and history. Lohman's grave is just a few hundred feet from the final resting place of Washington Irving. At the cemetery's main office, a map can be obtained for your visit.

JOSEPH BARBARA

"Joe the Barber"

During the late 1950s, organized crime was perceived as unorganized by most Americans. They had heard of unions of "families" controlled by bosses (dons) that had brought Old World heavy-handed discipline to the world of crime, but the magnitude of La Casa Nostra (literally "our thing"), or the Mafia, was unimagined. That is until "Joe the Barber" decided to throw a barbecue.

Joseph Barbara came from Sicily in 1920 as a teenager. In the post-prohibition era, he secured a major beer and soft drink distributorship in New York's Southern Tier, in Binghamton. A popular, yet relatively small-time "player" among the crime families of the East, he hosted a large gathering of Mafioso at his centrally located Apalachin, New York, home, which was right on the Pennsylvania border. He had suffered from heart problems and thought this gesture would alleviate any stresses of attending a family sit-down somewhere else on the East Coast.

On November 14, 1957, New York State Police Sgt. Edgar Croswell and Investigator Vincent Vasisko stumbled upon the Mob gathering while working on a totally unrelated case. They followed a long parade of shiny black automobiles to the rural estate and staked it out. Sensing they had come upon something big, they started writing down the license plate numbers of the cars and initiated a raid on the Barbara home. At the first sign of trouble, the crime bosses headed for the woods. Later, Croswell and Vasisko would regale the press with stories of a bunch of overweight grown men running through the woods in $1,000 Italian suits and black felt fedoras, all the while tossing large wads of money and guns into the woods and creeks along the property. Needless to say, all fifty-eight mobsters were caught. At the police barracks just down the road from the home, more than $300,000 in cash was emptied from the soiled and torn pockets of the out-of-breath crooks.

The lineup of names attending the crime summit surprised even the Feds. Every major crime figure in the East was there, including family heads Vito Genovese, Carlo Gambino, Joseph Bonanno, Joseph Profaci, and Paul Castellano. No crime had actually occurred, and no jail time was served (everyone said they were simply attending a casual barbecue at the home of a sick friend), but the press came alive with stories of the length and breadth of the crime syndication in the country, and there could no longer be a denial of the Mafia in America. This discovery embarrassed FBI head J. Edgar Hoover, and he attacked the Mob with a vengeance. The "Apalachin Raid" would go down as the beginning of the end for all of the players who were caught eating some of the three hundred steaks barbecued at Joe the Barber's place that autumn day.

Crime boss Barbara died of a heart attack at the age of fifty-five on June 17, 1959, and is buried in Johnson City, New York.

Author's note: Barbara is buried at Calvary-St. Patrick Cemetery. Leave NYS Route 17 at the exit to the sprawling Oakdale Mall and make your first right on Harry L. Drive. Just a few hundred feet down the road is the cemetery on your left, and you will enter at the first gate. Travel up this road (inside the cemetery) through four major intersections and stop. Most of the graves are marked with relatively low-rising stones.

Barbara's grave, however, is marked by one of the tallest monuments in this section and is readily recognized. A large dark cross behind a white marble Christ figure marks his grave. The gold letters along the bottom read BARBARA. His family is buried here with him. Barbara's grave is the northernmost plot in Section 14.

Items from Barbara's estate were auctioned off in August 2002. Hundreds attended, hoping to go home with a bit of Mob history, and many did. One of those there that day was Joseph Barbara's grandson. Items went for as much as $18,000 for a large hand-carved poker table to $80 for a small end table (purchased by New York news and sports radio broadcaster Jeff Bishop). The home (625 McFall Road) sold to Mrs. Susan Deakin of Connecticut for more than $300,000. And yes, the barbecue pit went with the house! The "Apalachin Raid" has been featured in several crime-themed movies, from a serious treatment in *Inside the Mafia* (1959) starring Cameron Mitchell to an appropriately hilarious depiction in *Analyze This* (1999) starring Billy Crystal and Robert DeNiro.

The five major crime family heads that attended the "Mob-e-que" are deceased. Paul Castellano (d. 1985) is buried in Moravian Cemetery, New Dorp, New York, and Joseph Profaci (d. 1967), Vito Genovese (d. 1969), and Carlo Gambino (d. 1976) are all buried in St. John's Cemetery (often called "the Mob's Boot Hill"), Middle Village, New York. Joseph Bonanno lived the longest (d. 2002) and is buried in Holy Hope Cemetery, Tucson, Arizona.

FATHER NELSON BAKER

"Padre of the Poor"

There is no more of an incongruous sight in all of New York than what the unsuspecting visitor to 767 Ridge Road finds in dreary, ordinary Lackawanna, New York. There stands a church rising gloriously over the suburban landscape. A majestic, towering cathedral unlike any in the whole world. The sight is jolting. Yet, this is no typical place of worship. This is a powerful symbol of faith, a monument to the memory of the life of a true servant of God. The church is the Basilica of Our Lady of Victory, and the man it memorializes is Father Nelson Baker: "The Padre of the Poor."

In 1882 when Father Baker became the head of St. John's Protectory (a Buffalo, New York, orphanage), he was shocked to hear of baby bones being unearthed along the muddy bottom of the newly built Erie Canal. He was determined to open the orphanage's doors to anyone who needed assistance, regardless of means or situation. He took in stray boys and gave them vocational training and founded an Infant Home that became the largest adoption center east of the Mississippi. He opened avenues of hope to hundreds of young girls when he established a Maternity Home for unwed mothers, and he provided learning centers for the handicapped, a segment of society quickly forgotten about in the late 1800s. It was Father Baker's intention to leave no need unfilled, and soon his charitable organization was the largest of its kind in the entire United States!

On a return trip from a papal visit in 1874, he stopped at the famous Shrine of Our Lady of Victory near Paris. The visit set into motion a dream of his to build a giant American shrine to the Blessed Mother that would rival any house of worship in the world. With the help of thousands of contributors worldwide, his dream came true in 1926. Father Baker's $3,000,000 cathedral has since been judged one of the most beautiful cathedrals anywhere. Guarded by four eighteen-foot angels, the building is awe-inspiring in its sweeping grandeur. Inside the great bronze doors are an exact replica of the Grotto of Lourdes, several priceless French stained-glass windows, imported African mahogany pews, life-sized marble statues of *all* the Apostles, and a 1,600-pound statue of Our Lady of Victory.

The declaration of a basilica denotes a place of "special beauty and historical significance," and the only way any church can be so deemed is by papal edict. Just two months after the completion of his "dream church," Father Baker witnessed its renaming by Pope Pius XI to the Basilica of Our Lady of Victory. It is only the second American church so honored.

Father Baker's Infant Home was always left unlocked at night, with an empty crib standing just inside the front door. Many desperate young mothers anonymously placed their babies in that crib, entrusting the care of their infants to Father Baker and his organization. To date, more than 50,000 orphans have passed through the doors of his Infant Home.

Father Nelson Baker died on July 29, 1936, at the age of ninety-five. President Franklin D. Roosevelt led the nation in mourning this "Apostle of Charity." Over a half-million people attended the funeral services at his basilica, a service that was officiated over by seven hundred priests. Many in the crowd of mourners that day were "Father Baker Boys," orphans who had received a second chance at life due to the kindness of the "Padre of the Poor."

In the summer of 1987, the Congregation for the Causes of the Saints approved the initiation of Father Baker's cause for sainthood and forever bestowed upon his name "Servant of God."

Author's note: Lackawanna is located in far-western New York State just south of Buffalo. The route to the basilica, at 767 Ridge Road, is well pointed by signs (in fact, so well-known and recognized is the story of this saintly man that the city limit signs at the edge of town read "Welcome to Lackawanna, N.Y., Home Of Father Nelson Baker, 'The Padre of the Poor'." The priest originally was buried in Holy Cross Cemetery, which abuts the cathedral. There were directional signs to his gravesite in Section A. The cemetery boasts "the graves of early Irish immigrants, those who dug the Erie Canal, built the railroads, worked the docks, and built the Great Lakes steamships." It is a sprawling area of acre after acre of lush plantings and shady trees. More than 150,000 graves dot the landscape. *But ...* Father Baker is no longer buried in the church cemetery. In 1999, in an effort to make his final resting place more accessible to the general public, it was decided to exhume his body and bury him inside the basilica under the front altar. Amazingly, the cemetery workers who dug up his coffin were stunned to find *two* coffins in his plot. Upon opening the smaller one, church officials found three mysterious vials of liquid. These sealed vials were taken to a laboratory for analysis, and it was discovered that they contained Father Baker's blood! Blood in liquid form after six decades! This finding no doubt moved the canonization of the most popular Catholic priest of the twentieth century farther down the road. Six elderly "Father Baker Boys" were summoned to carry the coffin of their mentor into the church and place it in its new resting place. For tour and general information, call the cathedral office at 716-828-9444. In 2001, the seventy-fifth anniversary of the cathedral, more than 25,000 made the trip to Lackawanna. Of special note is the date October 7th, when the entire large parish celebrates the Feast of Our Lady of Victory with much celebration (www.ourladyofvictory.org).

Admiral John L. Worden_____

"The Monitor and the Merrimack"

Admiral John Worden was one of the greatest of all the legendary U.S. Navy heroes.

Born in 1818 at Ossining, New York (a historical plaque marks the spot on Route 9 in the town), he went on to become one of the most storied military leaders of the Civil War. After being captured and held by the South for nearly seven months during the war, President Lincoln rewarded Worden with the prestigious assignment of helming the experimental metal-clad ship *Monitor*. Fitted with impenetrable steel sheathing, she was the technological marvel of her day. Not to be outdone, the Confederates scuttled a 4,600-ton frigate named *Merrimack* and transformed it into the *CSS Virginia* (although a confusing naval tradition holds that the ship be referred to by its original name). On March 9, 1862, all eyes were on Hampton Roads, Virginia, where the two iron giants of the sea met in combat for the first time. Admiral Worden was severely wounded during the ferocious engagement and was evacuated from his *Monitor*. The two ships fought to a stalemate, and both survived, albeit dented and misshapen from the cannon shot. It was the first battle of ironclad ships in history, and it ushered in a new phase of naval warfare.

Admiral Worden was a personal friend and confidant of Abraham Lincoln, and his patron gladly repaid the naval officer's heroism by naming him in 1868 to the highest-ranking position in the service, commodore. One year later, he was named superintendent of the United States Naval Academy. During his four-year term at the academy, he was made rear admiral.

He died in 1897 and was buried in Pawling Cemetery, Route 22, Pawling, New York.

Author's note: Admiral Worden's grave is unmistakable in this small cemetery. With a five-foot-tall anchor carved across a huge, rough boulder, his final resting place is a moving testament to his naval legacy. A brass plaque at the entrance to the cemetery tells of his heroics during the "Battle of the Ironclads." This is a small but quite beautiful cemetery. Former New York State governor and presidential nominee Thomas E. Dewey is also buried here in a large mausoleum.

Fort Worden State Park in Washington State honors the admiral, as does Worden Field, the large parade ground at the U.S. Naval Academy.

Worden's ship, *Monitor*, sank in a terrible storm off Cape Hatteras, North Carolina, on New Year's Eve, 1862. Four of its officers and twelve crewmen died. The remains of the ship were discovered on the floor of the Atlantic Ocean over a century later. A salvage operation went into effect in 1973, and some of the ship's items were salvaged and put on display at the Mariner's Museum in Newport News, Virginia. The biggest story happened only recently. On August 5, 2002, after a months-long recovery effort and more than six million dollars spent, the *Monitor's* large intact gun turret was found and brought to the surface. This is the most significant and final artifact of the ship, and it is considered to be one of the most historic finds ever recovered from the deep. The nine-foot-tall, 160-ton turret was discovered to be in excellent condition and will take more than a decade to restore. "We'll take it apart piece by piece, bolt by bolt," said Chris Peterson, director of the museum. "Eventually all of the rust, marine encrustations and corrosive salt will be removed and the turret will be pieced back together and put on permanent display. It is a national treasure." A new wing of the Mariner's Museum will be constructed around 2007 and will house only the artifacts recovered from the *Monitor* (including the turret). Some of the many items include the ship's anchor, lanterns, a ship's ladder, some salt and pepper shakers, thermometers, and a large piece of porcelain with the word "PUSH" on it. It is thought to be part of the ship's toilet!

The glory of the Confederate ship *Merrimack* ended shortly after Hampton Roads. It was sunk so as not to be captured by the North. During World War I, the U.S. Navy mistook the hulking remains of the Civil War-era ship to be those of a prowling German submarine. The navy promptly blasted the remains with depth charges and sent the pieces scattering over a large area of the ocean floor, never to be recovered.

From Pawling Cemetery, I would encourage all readers to take the five-minute side trip up Route 22, which is across the street from the entrance to the cemetery. This leads you up to Quaker Hill, a delightful and beautiful mountaintop crossroads. At the four corners at the top of the hill, you will see a strikingly handsome old church on your right. To the right of this church, you will notice a large rose-colored boulder with a plaque on it. This is the grave of famed journalist Lowell Thomas. The rambling old farmhouse across the road from the church is the former home of Norman Vincent Peale. The luxuriously rustic horse farm down the block from the four corners belonged to Congressman Hamilton Fish, a member of one of the most famous political families in New York history. Across the road and down a couple of blocks, you will find the magnificent home of the late newsman Edward R. Murrow. You will not find Murrow's grave up on Quaker Hill, however. He was cremated and his ashes were scattered over the mountaintop.

DR. MARY E. WALKER

"Only Female Medal of Honor Winner"

Mary Edwards Walker was born in Oswego, New York, in 1832. Her parents were stern non-believers who preached that their children should not adhere to the normal practices of life when the urge to be different presented itself to them. Her parents were active abolitionists (it is important to note that there are a dozen registered Underground Railroad sites in and around Oswego County), and the family home was a lively center for political discussion and debate. Her father believed that his many daughters were encumbered by tight-fitting "women clothes," which hampered their movement and work ability. In her younger years, Mary would forever swear off female clothing and would dress in a masculine style throughout the rest of her life. When she got married in 1864, she wore a man's suit and (daringly) refused to take her new husband's name! She was one of the first females to enter Syracuse Medical College (1855) and emerged as the first female graduate of that school and only the second female graduate of a medical school in America (six years behind Elizabeth Blackwell).

During the Civil War, Mary Walker was appointed Assistant Surgeon in the Union Army. She tended to the battlefield wounds of her charges while exposing herself to enemy fire on numerous occasions. One time, she was captured and held prisoner by the South. Four months later, she and sixteen Union doctors were part of a prisoner exchange involving twenty-four Confederate surgeons. Confederate sources pegged Dr. Walker as a spy and had placed a large bounty on her head.

For her wartime heroics, Dr. Mary Edwards Walker was awarded the Congressional Medal of Honor. To this day, she is the first and only female recipient of this prestigious award.

After the war, Mary became a follower of Amelia Bloomer and the radical women's dress movement, which wanted to change the perception of women as "dress wearers" and put them on a more equal "attire footing" with men. (Bloomer, also from Upstate New York, gave her name to "bloomers," a masculine pantaloon that was the counterpart to men's trousers.) Dr. Walker was a quirky and eccentric personality, and she gave many speeches and talks before large audiences and at rural carnivals.

In 1917, two years before her death, the U.S. government changed pension and medal rules. Dr. Walker's pension was rescinded, and her Congressional Medal of Honor was instructed to be handed back. (This 1917 ruling was implemented to correct over nine hundred Medal of Honor awards that were considered "unofficial." In fact, some early award winners were given the medal as an enticement to re-enlist! This purge was an effort to elevate the presentation of the Congressional Medal of Honor to its rightful prestigious place.) Dr. Walker fought ferociously for her pension and was reinstated at $20 per month. She simply refused to give her medal back and instead wore it proudly every day for the rest of her life. When she died, Mary Walker was buried in Oswego's Rural Cemetery wearing a man's suit *and* her Congressional Medal of Honor!

Author's note: Oswego sits hard on Lake Ontario in northwestern New York State. Dr. Walker is remembered fondly here through commemorations and events. The site of her home on Bunker Hill Road is marked by a New York State historical marker. When the government issued a postage stamp in Walker's memory on June 10, 1982, a special event was held at the local post office.

The cemetery is located in the Fruit Valley section of the Town of Oswego. Travel out of the city on Route 104 (west past SUNY Oswego) and make a left at the light (Cemetery Road). Go straight into the cemetery through the main entrance and stop at the second set of steps on your right. On the rise, you will see the military gravesite of Dr. Walker. It is adorned with the Medal of Honor insignia. In October of 2000, Dr. Mary Walker was enshrined in the Women's Hall of Fame in Seneca Falls, New York, as the "Nation's only female Medal of Honor winner and the nation's second female graduate of a medical college." In 1977, President Jimmy Carter reinstated Dr. Mary Edwards Walker's Congressional Medal of Honor saying, "Her distinguished gallantry, self-sacrifice and unflinching loyalty to country were evident despite the apparent discrimination because of her sex."

John Burroughs

"The Sage of Slabsides"

John Burroughs was a simple man with spartan tastes. He dressed casually (some would say raggedly) and sported a chin full of flowing white whiskers. He trudged lonely forgotten country roads as if a man on a mission. For seventy-five years, he was a familiar, solitary figure along the dusty back roads of the northern Catskill Mountains of Upstate New York. A study in contradictions, Burroughs' rough-hewn demeanor masked a keen mind and a deft sense of purpose. Having been brought up in an area he compared to "paradise," he was determined to become one with nature and to preserve for the future the beauty of the land he so loved.

Born in rural Roxbury, New York, the young Burroughs would climb the hilltop behind his home and gaze out across the pristine valleys from his favorite vantage spot, "Boyhood Rock." It was from this viewpoint that America's greatest naturalist first came under the spell of Mother Nature and her wondrous talents. His first essays, written while he was still only in his twenties, captured the imagination of his reading audience immediately, and he soon decided that he was meant to be a writer.

Burroughs found that being a writer meant infrequent paydays and empty cupboards, so in 1869, to support his young family, he made a fateful move from the wilderness of Upstate New York to the bustle of our nation's capital, Washington, D.C. Although the job he landed was mundane (a clerk at the Currency Bureau), a chance meeting with his idol, Walt Whitman, changed the course of Burroughs' life forever. The two men became inseparable friends, and a tutorial relationship grew out of their mutual admiration and respect. Burroughs would later reflect that he owed much of his career to the teachings of "Master Whitman." In tribute, he published *Notes on Walt Whitman as Poet and Person* in 1867. In 1871, his first great nature study, *Wake Robin*, was published (friend Whitman suggested the title). The book was favorably reviewed by the critics, and his future works were eagerly anticipated.

Burroughs' prose and poetry were provocative, passionate, and prolific. His writing output was astonishing: *Locusts and Wild Honey* (1879), *Signs and Seasons* (1886), *Leaf and Tendril* (1880), *The Summit of the Years* (1913), *Under the Apple Trees* (1916), and *Field and Study* (1919) were all major Burroughs' works. For the last forty years of his life, he averaged one book every two years! In all, he sold 1,500,000 copies of his twenty-three books.

Although he disdained the outward trappings of fame and notoriety, many of the great personages of his era sought audience with him for both advice and friendship. He even camped with President Theodore Roosevelt at Yosemite! He was heralded as the "Father of the American Conservation Movement," and even in his final years, his speaking schedule was enough to tire a younger man.

Having traveled to California in the spring of 1921 to fulfill a speaking commitment, he suddenly fell ill and, perhaps sensing that the end was near, directed that he be transported to his Catskill

Mountain home as quickly as possible. He never made it. On March 29, 1921, he died on a train heading east. He was just shy of his eighty-fourth birthday.

John Burroughs is buried behind his rustic home, "Woodchuck Lodge," on Hardscrabble Road just east of Roxbury, New York (off NYS Route 30).

Author's note: As rural as his gravesite sounds, New York State has wisely marked the area with many informative signs and photos of Burroughs' life. Hundreds travel to Woodchuck Lodge each year to visit his final resting place, behind the lodge, beneath Boyhood Rock. Usually a tin box is lying along the stone wall surrounding his grave. Inside are notes from nature lovers from all over the world who have left their thoughts. A pencil is usually left alongside, and you are encouraged to leave your own message. The lodge received an excellent twenty-first-century facelift in the spring of 2005 by Furlan and Sons of Milford, New York, historic restorers.

His official home, "Slabsides," is located in West Park, New York, along the Hudson River. The cabin, built in 1895, and the 180-acre nature sanctuary next to it are located between Highland and Kingston, New York. In West Park, go up Floyd Ackert Road a half-mile. Park and follow the signs up the hill to Slabsides. There are two open houses a year held here, one on the third Saturday in May and the other on the first Saturday in October. On these days, many attend to witness the splendor of springtime and autumn in the Hudson Valley. Inside you can see photos of the famous visitors who came to commiserate with Burroughs: Walt Whitman, Henry Ford, Thomas Edison, and others. His old straw hat still hangs on the peg by the door.

A permanent display devoted to Burroughs is located at the American Museum of Natural History in New York City. He recently was named among the six initial charter members of the Ecology Hall of Fame, with Rachel Carson, Henry David Thoreau, John Muir, Alan Chadwick, and Aldo Leopold. A permanent Ecology Hall of Fame and Museum is being planned for a site near Monterey Bay, California (www.ecotopia.org).

John W. "Bud" Fowler

"Before Jackie Robinson…1ˢᵗ Black in Baseball!"

Nearly seventy years before Jackie Robinson broke the "visible" color line in baseball, Bud Fowler broke the "invisible" one.

At the dawning of the baseball era, there were no racial restrictions in professional baseball. It was a white man's game, and few men of color even dared think about facing the gauntlet of racial scorn they would have to endure by joining professional baseball in late 1800s' America. John Fowler was the *first* documented black man to don a professional baseball uniform. He was a talented and aggressive player who put serious numbers on his stat sheet. Another serious number he reached was twenty. That is the number of teams he played for—in ten years. As a black man in a white man's game, Fowler was a man on the move.

Born John Jackson (nobody really knows why he changed his name to Bud Fowler), he played for the Keokuks in the Western League in 1885. There would be many blacks in minor league baseball from the start (1877), but Bud Fowler was the first (and the best) to make the big time. A short (five foot seven), wiry spitfire of a man, he threw and batted right-handed. In seven of his ten years as a player, he batted over .300. Although he played every position on the field with prowess, he was considered the best second baseman in the league, and he was a feared base runner. His exploits on the diamond stirred the racial insecurities of his white, Southern audiences, and team after team traded him for "safety reasons." At the turn of the century, when "whites only" became the official rule of the game, Fowler played for and managed many black teams in the Negro Leagues.

In 1894, he founded the famous Page Fence Giants. This all-black team was sponsored by the Page Woven Wire Fence Company of Adrian, Michigan. They traveled America playing before large crowds and were a commercial success. With this success came the trappings of fame. They traveled in a comfortable, custom-made railroad car, equipped with a commercial kitchen and plush sleeping quarters. Cooks, servants, and porters catered to their every need. Large crowds would usually welcome them to their playing engagements. Bud Fowler became the first black baseball celebrity.

He never saw Jackie Robinson smash through baseball's color line in 1947. Fowler died in 1913 at the age of fifty-four. He is buried in Oak View Cemetery, Frankfort, New York.

Author's note: Although he was the first notable black professional baseball player, Fowler rested in anonymity for decades. His unmarked grave was a sad footnote to his courageous and exciting life. In an attempt to bring attention to this forgotten sports legend, the Society for American Baseball Research bought and paid for a modest marble stone for his gravesite in 1987. It reads: "Bud Fowler. Black Baseball Pioneer."

To get to his grave, drive six miles east of Utica, New York, and exit at Frankfort Fairground (Exit 58). Make a left on Higby Road, and the cemetery is less than a mile down the road. Enter Oak View Cemetery at the second (northern) gate. John (Bud Fowler) Jackson's gravestone is halfway down the road on the right. It is just past the large, stone mausoleum. While leaving the cemetery, notice the Balloon House on its southern boundary. A cluster of New York State historical markers tell the fascinating story of the house's former inhabitants, Carlotta and Carl Myers. Carlotta was America's foremost "lady aeronaut," and her pioneering balloon ascensions in the late 1800s were national news. The village of Frankfort has much in local history and lore. William Gates's match factory in town created the first of millions of the now-common friction match. He sold his invention and company to Diamond Matches and made a fortune.

RUSSELL SAGE

"The Money King"

"Any man can earn a dollar, but it takes a *wise* man to save it."

Russell Sage once boasted that he had "the first dollar he ever earned" and he lived by his "Saving Golden Rule" all of his life. When he died in 1906, he darned near had every dollar he ever made. Well, at least ninety million of them!

A true Wall Street titan, Sage dealt with all of the great moneymen and financiers of his era, including his good friend Jay Gould. He amassed a huge fortune, first as a successful merchant and then as a money manager on Wall Street. As a railroad tycoon, he once boasted that he was president of twenty different railroads *simultaneously*!

Sage was a teetotaler of simple habits who married the love of his life in 1840, eighteen-year-old Marie-Henri Winne. Uncharacteristically, Sage adored his beautiful young wife uncritically. When she died unexpectedly at the age of forty-five, he grieved deeply. He would mourn his sweet Marie-Henri for the rest of his own long life.

Although he spent time as a U.S. congressman, he was a recluse by nature. His devotion to his businesses kept him behind closed doors and insulated him from the outside world through most of his Wall Street career. One startling episode, however, thrust Sage onto the front pages of every newspaper in America and changed his life forever.

On December 4, 1891, a disgruntled investor came to Sage's Wall Street office in an attempt to extort money from the millionaire. By mistake, a bomb the man was carrying blew up right in front of Sage. The intruder was blown out the window to his death on the street below. Sage's longtime clerk was also killed, and eight others were seriously injured. Sage himself walked out of his office unscathed.

One of the injured employees, clerk William Laidlaw, asked Sage to cover the cost of his hospitalization. The tight-fisted financier refused to make payment, and Laidlaw took his former boss to court. At the proceedings, the clerk testified that at the moment of the bomb blast Sage had thrown Laidlaw in front of him. This public accusation of cowardice enraged Sage, and he vowed that the clerk "would never receive a cent!" Although Laidlaw sued for a modest amount ($25,000), Sage mounted a major legal offensive. The trial lasted seven years and cost Sage $100,000. Needless to say, he was victorious. Shortly after the trial, Laidlaw died penniless.

In 1869, aware that it was a social necessity for a man of his stature to have a wife, Sage made a marriage of convenience to one Margaret Olivia Slocum. She was an austere and rigid woman whose regal bearing would hide a soon-to-be-revealed heart of gold.

On July 22, 1906, Russell Sage died at the ripe old age of ninety. Few mourned the passing of the once-powerful "Money King." Now the richest woman on Wall Street, Sage's widow immediately began distributing the tycoon's wealth. To her eternal credit, she was benevolent on an unprecedented scale. In total, she donated almost *all* of her late husband's fortune in just over ten years. Of the nearly $75,000,000 dispensed, a college in Troy, New York, was one of the major beneficiaries. Fittingly, it is called Russell Sage College.

Author's note: Fearing that her husband's body would be dug up and held for ransom, his wife ordered bizarre measures to prevent a grave robbing at his tomb. The diminutive millionaire was buried in a massive *six-ton* coffin that cost $22,000 and took twenty-five men to lift. His mausoleum at Oakwood Cemetery in Troy is a scale replica of the ancient Parthenon. It carries no identifying family names or marks, and is equipped with a burglar alarm. Marie-Henri Winne, the only person to ever reach the crusty old miser's heart during his ninety years on earth, rests in a separate grave right next to his. To reach the cemetery, travel north on Oakwood Avenue (off Route 7, known as Hoosick Street in the city) in Troy one mile north of Frear Park. Enter the main gate and proceed through the cemetery. Make your first major right-hand turn and you will see, on your right, the giant columned mausoleum of "The Money King." Many famous people are buried in this cemetery, and the main office will gladly give you a map highlighting the various interesting stops along a cemetery tour.

An interesting side note is the fact that the widow Sage financed a new campus for education pioneer Emma Willard in Troy in 1910. Emma Willard is also buried in this cemetery. So is Amos Eaton, co-founder of the Rensselaer Polytechnic Institute, which he began in 1824. R.P.I. is the nation's oldest technological university.

MARGARET CORBIN

"Captain Molly"

The long and somber rows of gravestones at West Point speak reverently and eloquently of the enormous sacrifices made to keep America free. Representatives of all wars are commingled here in a common ground of honor. But one gravesite, set far apart from all the others, tells a most unusual tale of courage under fire and unselfish sacrifice to her fellow soldiers. The stone, standing a silent vigil under a towering shade tree, is that marking the final resting place of Margaret Corbin, the legendary Revolutionary War heroine known as "Captain Molly."

During the war, Margaret's husband, John Corbin, served as an artillery officer. Margaret (known as Molly) would accompany her husband to various battle stations where she would spend her time nursing the wounded and cooking for the soldiers. During the fierce fight against the Hessians at the Battle of Fort Washington (New York City) on November 16, 1776, John Corbin took a mortal wound from enemy fire. Witnessing her husband's death, Molly courageously took over his cannon emplacement and continued to direct shelling toward the enemy. Eventually, she too was cut down by a rifle shot. Although she was not killed, her wounds were so severe that one arm was nearly severed. Perhaps in noble recognition of her gallant bravery, the victorious Hessians refused to take Captain Molly prisoner and instead freed her to return to her native Pennsylvania. Her heroic actions had earned her the respect and admiration of combatants on both sides of the field of battle.

The remainder of Molly Corbin's life was spent petitioning the Board of War and the U.S. Congress for battlefield compensation. Totally incapacitated, she was finally awarded just $30 per month in relief benefits on June 29, 1779. Later, Congress granted her a lifetime pension amounting to "one-half the pay of a soldier in service."

Embittered by the trauma of early widowhood and a lifetime of physical hardship (exacerbated by her terrible war injuries), she began to drink heavily and sank into a life of reclusive eccentricity. When she died at age forty-eight, she was an impoverished, disliked, forgotten woman whose legendary actions had all but been blotted out.

Buried in an unmarked grave in Highland Falls, New York, her remains were re-interred at West Point with full honors in 1926 (following an examination of her wartime heroics by the Daughters of the American Revolution). At this time, it was also officially noted that not only was Captain Molly Corbin an original American heroine, but she was also documented as the *first* woman to receive a government pension in the U.S.!

Author's note: The hallowed grounds of the U.S. Military Academy Cemetery at West Point, New York, are a popular highlight of a tour of this historic facility. Captain Molly is buried behind the Old Chapel under a giant shade tree. There is a bronze plaque telling the story of her heroic actions at the Battle of Fort Washington. You are well advised to make a stop at the West Point gift shop and obtain a free map of the cemetery grounds, where you will see featured the gravesites of General George Armstrong Custer, Major General George Goethals (builder of the Panama Canal), astronaut Edward

H. White (first man to walk in space), Major General Frederick Dent Grant (President U.S. Grant's son), and many other military luminaries.

Molly Corbin is also remembered at the site of her heroics. There, in present-day Fort Tryon Park, in Manhattan (near 190th Street), you will find a statue and gardens placed in her honor on the former battlefield of the Battle of Fort Washington (the area is known as Washington Heights). This park, considered by many to be one of the most beautiful parks in New York City, offers stunning views of the Hudson River, George Washington Bridge, and the cliffs fringing the New Jersey side.

On another note, there was some early controversy as to who the *real* Captain Molly was. After much examination of records, the other contender, Mary (Molly) McCauley, was deemed to be "Molly Pitcher," a heroine of the Battle of Monmouth who served water from a pitcher to the wounded. The Monmouth County Library in Manalapan, New Jersey, put the search for both Mollys into a popular exhibit.

CLAYTON BATES

"Peg Leg"

Clayton Bates was born on October 11, 1907. His parents were dirt-poor sharecroppers from Fountain Inn, South Carolina, and Clayton began working to help support the family at the age of twelve. On only his second day at the job at the local mill, he suffered a terrible accident that would change his life forever … for the good!

A sudden power outage plunged the mill into darkness, and young Clayton stumbled onto a sugar-grinding conveyor belt, which jolted into action when the power surged back on. Unable to escape, his left leg was mangled beyond repair. In those days of segregated hospitals in the South and no medical insurance for the poor black workers, Clayton's bleeding body was simply carried to his family home, where a neighbor amputated his left leg at the knee. This surgery was performed on his mother's kitchen table.

At the time of his accident, Clayton had been doing very well with a side business of street performing. A natural rhythmist, he was an acrobatic tap dancer who had made pennies and nickels dancing for the local townspeople on the sidewalks of Fountain Inn since the age of five. He desperately wanted to continue this hobby after the accident and forced himself to recover and rehabilitate with great speed. Within two months of having his leg taken off, he was on his feet and walking with the aid of two crutches made out of broomsticks. Shortly after this, his uncle whittled Clayton a wooden leg and strapped it onto his left leg stump. Clayton called it his "peg leg" and the name stuck. Within six months of his accident, Peg Leg was walking and running on his new leg and began performing his tap dance routines once more. With one leg.

Peg Leg Bates's unusual dance style (he pounded out the drum cadence of the beat with his wooden leg) drew attention from far and wide. An affable artist with a soaring spirit, Peg Leg devised outlandish feats of tap dancing that drew standing-room-only crowds wherever he went. He was a first-rate draw on the minstrel circuit and eventually caught the eye of the major promoters of his era. He was booked into the famed Cotton Club in Harlem for three weeks in the 1930s, and his fame became secured. His show-stopping move was an improvised dance step that always brought the crowd to its feet, cheering and applauding wildly. He called the step the "Imitation American Jet Plane Jump." It called for him to jump his own height (more than five feet) spin crazily in the air, and then land on his wooden leg with a tremendous thump, while sticking his good leg straight out behind him. It was an act that took him to the greatest concert halls in the world and even persuaded the queen of England to ask for a command performance. It was also an act that would reduce Bates to a whimpering, pain-wracked heap in his dressing room many times after a show.

Bates made a fortune from dancing and lived a very comfortable life. He and his family lived in good homes and drove fancy cars. He owned thirteen custom-made peg legs ("one for each color of suit he owned") and became a supporter of many social causes. He performed twenty-two times on the *Ed Sullivan Show*, more than any other dancer. Once, while performing at Grossinger's Resort in the Catskill Mountains of New York, he noticed that all of the audiences he performed to were still totally white (as they were in his early days of segregated vaudeville), and he decided to open a resort in the mountains for African-American audiences. In 1951, he turned his sixty-acre farm in Kerhonkson, New York, into Peg Leg Bates' Country Club and ran it quite successfully for nearly forty years. Here he would greet his customers at the front door, sign autographs, and smile for hundreds of pictures. And he also performed there regularly.

Peg Leg Bates officially retired from show business in 1989, but he never stayed "off-stage" for long. He spoke to countless civic groups about racial harmony, rights for the disabled, and the problems found with disadvantaged young people. He was a motivational speaker of eloquence and sincerity.

In his final years, Peg Leg Bates was honored as a superior talent by many in the entertainment industry. Young dancers found their way to him, and he basked in their admiration. His incredible journey was depicted in several television specials and books. Finally, he was awarded the Order of the Palmetto, the highest civilian award given out in his native South Carolina. He called it the proudest moment of his life.

A drive was underway in Fountain Inn to raise money to erect a life-sized statue of Bates on the steps of Fountain Inn's City Hall. On Saturday night, December 5, 1998, he was honored at a special fund-raising event, and at the end he performed one of his trademark dances, peg leg and all. The following morning, while walking to church, he dropped dead of a heart attack. He was ninety-one years old.

Peg Leg Bates is buried in Palentown Cemetery, in Ulster County, New York.

Author's note: Of the many entries in *Great Graves* there are two that are special to me. These are the people that I actually knew or met. One is the great Kate Smith, whom I first met when I was seventeen years old in 1967. It was an odd pairing, me the "young hippie wanderer" and she the older "First Lady of Radio," but she was a fun lady, and I enjoyed watching her perform, especially "God Bless America." The other person that I actually met was Peg Leg Bates.

In late 1988, I was invited to attend the dedication of the new multimillion dollar library on the campus of the State University of New York at Delhi (NY). I had sung the national anthem for sporting events and gatherings for a number of years at the college and was asked to sing at the ceremony. My good friend Gary Cole, an administrator at the college, told me, "Chuck, you will be sitting on the main stage next to a *very* interesting gentleman." This cryptic message certainly caught my interest.

On the day of the gathering, hundreds assembled in the giant gymnasium for the ceremony. I was seated at the very end of a very long dais. Next to me sat a large elderly black man with a wooden leg. I soon learned it was Peg Leg Bates! After I sang, I returned to my seat, where Peg Leg turned to me and whispered, "Good job on that song, sir." I smiled.

At the end of the ceremony, it was announced that Peg Leg Bates was being awarded an honorary degree from the college. The president of SUNY Delhi listed all of his credits and achievements before calling him to the podium. I could see in the sea of faces of the hundreds of young students looking up at the stage that same look that must have been seen by Peg Leg for over eighty years. A look that said, "A one-legged tap dancer?" At the end of the speech, I leaned over and gently pulled his chair back and helped him to his feet. Dressed nattily in a black silk three-piece suit, he tucked his crutch under his arm and went to receive his award. After, he told the audience, in a gentle whisper, of how proud he was to get this honor and how wonderful his life had been. He reminded the students that there are no real barriers or obstacles in the road of life, only opportunities. He reflected that if he could become a star with all that was thrown at him since childhood, then certainly *anybody* could make it. He bowed and thanked the gathering and began to return to his seat. And then something amazing began to take place. Slowly at first, and then louder and more forcefully, a clap began to ring throughout the gymnasium. "CLAP! CLAP! CLAP! CLAP! ..."

He turned to the huge crowd and gazed out over the young faces, finally realizing that they were clapping and chanting for him. A broad smile creased his face, and he slowly turned and went back to the speaker's podium. "I suppose you want to see this old one-legged tap dancer do his thing, don't you?" A cheer went up. He chuckled and stepped back. Everyone rose in silence to watch him take a couple of seconds to prepare. I looked around and saw hundreds standing and craning their necks to get a look. All of the assembled dignitaries on the stage were also standing, including the president of the university and the lieutenant governor of the State of New York. And then from the silence it began. A gentle tapping at first, almost like a knocking at a door. Then the thuds became more pronounced and the arms started twitching a little bit. His good leg began to shuffle out a tempo while his crutch kept time and his peg leg beat out a bass. Soon the years began to strip away as the master could be heard humming a song into the microphone, suit jacket flailing wildly as a crescendo of almost a century's worth of joy came bursting out of this legendary figure. At the dramatic end, he held his pose like in the old days, broke into an enormous smile, threw his arms out, stuck his peg leg out above the crowd, and swept the stage with a floor-dusting bow. The huge crowd, with an average age of perhaps just twenty years old, exploded in a tumultuous roar of approval.

The old man collected himself and slowly walked back to his seat next to me and sat down. I leaned over and got close to his sweaty, beaming face and whispered, "Good job on that dance, sir."

He winked at me and chuckled. "Thanks, man."

Bates's grave is remarkable. Located in a rural, remote region of the Catskill Mountains (Town of Rochester, near Samsonville), Palentown is merely a small cluster of homes at a country crossroads near the Ashokan Reservoir. Take Route 28 to 28A to Route 3. Turn right on Palentown Road and go less than a half-mile up the road to the cemetery. Enter at the second entrance and go around the curve to your left. Bates's black polished grave marker is on your left.

I have seen dozens and dozens of creative grave markings in my travels, but this one beats them all. On the front of the gravestone is a most astonishing depiction of Peg Leg and his wife on riding lawn mowers in front of their old nightclub. You can plainly see the dog wagging his tail, the cat's-eye glasses on his wife, the old Schaefer Beer signs in the club windows, and, yes, the wooden leg! Exit the cemetery and go up Palentown Road a mile or so and you will follow the signs to the Mountain Valley Resort–Peg Leg Bates' Country Club. It is a ghostly collection of dilapidated single-story buildings, an unfilled swimming pool, a desolate picnic area, and a woebegone nightclub. It doesn't appear to have been in operation for years, although a neighbor said it is sporadically used for parties. Despite the dreariness of the facility, it is not impossible to close one's eyes and imagine the sight, say, fifty years ago. They say at the time that busload after busload of tourists, mostly black, would clog the tiny, winding mountain roads, bringing masses of happy visitors to Peg

Leg's place. You can visualize the barbecue pit crowded with gaudily dressed vacationers, and the parking lot filled with old giant station wagons, the kind with the luggage carriers on top. And if you listen real hard, on a quiet Catskill Mountain evening, you may even hear the rhythmic thumping emanating from out of the clubhouse, as the ghost of Peg Leg Bates beats out rhythms to beat the band.

Oh, what a time it must have been.

JANE McCREA

"Tragic Bride of Fort Edward"

Jane McCrea was a beautiful, well-liked twenty-four-year-old woman living in the quiet region of rural Upstate New York when the battles of the Revolutionary War darkened her idyllic life. She was engaged to Lt. David Jones, a senior officer with the British troops under the command of General Burgoyne. Because of her close relationship with a British officer, McCrea was afforded a somewhat "protective status" by the British. On July 27th, her intended wedding day, McCrea and a friend, Sarah McNeil, were riding in the forest when they were kidnapped by Indians loyal to Burgoyne. One took McCrea, and the other took Mrs. McNeil. By the time McNeil got to the fort, McCrea was nowhere to be found. Thinking that their "protective status" would prevent them from being harmed, Mrs. McNeil was shocked when two Indian scouts arrived bearing a scalp. She knew in an instant that her young friend had been murdered by the Indians.

Lt. Jones was heartbroken and demanded severe action against the Indians. Burgoyne, in the unenviable position of having to arrest (and therefore alienate) his Indian compatriots, chose to do nothing. Various reports declared that McCrea had been shot in error by the British, murdered and scalped by the Indians, or even shot by the Americans during the pursuit. The only real fact was that she *was* scalped.

News of Jane McCrea's murder swept the region, portrayed as an act of betrayal by the British and an act of savagery by the Indians. The story of the doomed "Bride of Fort Edward" was told and retold all along the northern battlefront of New York. Long lines of volunteers stood in line to march with the colonists in her name. Troops from as far away as the Green Mountains of Vermont came to stand with the patriots. This great surge in troop strength proved to be the ultimate downfall of the indecisive Burgoyne when he was soundly defeated by these same troops several months later at the Battle of Saratoga, the defining turning point in the war.

The date of Jane McCrea's murder was July 27, 1777. She was buried in her wedding dress two miles from her home in Fort Edward, New York.

Author's note: The entire Lake George–Hudson Falls region of Upstate New York is fertile ground for those interested in Revolutionary War lore and history (with the decisive Saratoga Battlefield just minutes away). Battlefields, historical markers, and preserved sites dot the entire region. Jane McCrea was buried and re-interred three times. Her final resting place is in Union Cemetery, on Route 4, between Hudson Falls and Fort Edward, New York (just north of Albany). Her original gravestone, now more than two centuries old, is plainly visible from the highway and is encased in glass to protect it from the elements. The epitaph reads, in part: "Here rests the remains of Jane McCrea, age (unknown) and murdered by a band of Indians while on a visit to a relative (around AD 1777). Commemorating one of the most thrilling incidents in the annals of the American Revolution." This may *not* have been the truth, the whole truth, and nothing but the truth. Despite the fact that she was buried and re-buried three times, no proof remained of her certain cause of death. In 2004, The History Channel (and later the Discovery Channel) aired a full-length television documentary on the death of Jane McCrea and the hunt for facts relating to her murder. DNA experts were called in, distant family members of McCrea and McNeil (who survived the kidnapping but was later buried with McCrea) were located, and science was loosed upon this ages-old controversy. To make matters worse, it was discovered that some of McCrea's bones were missing, perhaps stolen during one of the many interments by souvenir hunters. The DNA trail definitively pointed to the remains of Sarah McNeil as one of the occupants of the grave. Two more distinct sets of remains were discovered. Nobody has ever claimed to have identified the *third* body, and no record of a third burial exists. As for poor Jane, the results showed that yes, in fact, she had been … well, on second thought, let's not spoil a good mystery!

The results can be found in the documentary *The Buried Secrets of the Revolutionary War*, originally done for The History Channel and then later aired on the Discovery Channel (December 2004 and early 2005). The program is repeated often, and you may order a copy of the show from their Website. For another dramatic insight into the fate Jane McCrea met on her intended wedding day, go online and research John Vanderlyn's exciting painting *The Death of Jane McCrea* (1804). It is considered a masterpiece and is not for the squeamish!

ANDREW CARNEGIE

"Richest Man in the World"

Andrew Carnegie was a man who had everything. Once "the richest man in the world," he displayed one of the most consistent runs of financial luck in the annals of American business history. He was a millionaire many times over by the age of thirty and would come as close to becoming America's first billionaire as anyone could. And yet he was a restive man, a man unsatisfied with the game of wealth building, which was played so ruthlessly by his nineteenth-century contemporaries. At the age of sixty-five, he made a decision to give his fortune away, piece by piece. *All of it!* And ... he almost did it!

The biography of Andrew Carnegie has been told and retold many times over the years. We all know that he was born in Scotland and came to this country at the age of twelve. Raised in stark poverty, the young Carnegie was a quick student who possessed an ambitious nature. He started work as a five-dollars-a-month bobbin-boy in a local (Pittsburgh, Pennsylvania) cotton factory. In quick succession, he rose to office manager, then telegraph operator, and finally assistant to the president of the Pennsylvania Railroad. He lived a spartan life and invested his salary wisely. One of his earliest investments was in the fledgling American steel industry. As the U.S. Industrial Revolution roared along, his investment soon doubled and then tripled and eventually led to the ownership of a large steel company. A tight-fisted and shrewd financier, he soon was the top producer of steel in America, and as the country began to grow up and out, his own fortunes grew to unheard-of heights.

Carnegie had a Midas touch, and his ensuing investments amassed him hundreds of millions of dollars. In one uncharacteristic setback, he mishandled a labor strike at a company mill, and the Homestead Steel Company riot in 1892 would haunt him for the rest of his life. In January of 1901, when he sold his steel empire to J.P. Morgan for half a billion dollars, the story was that at the closing of the deal Morgan, in his tall silk top hat and formal tails, turned to Carnegie, stuck out his hand, and said, "Congratulations, Mr. Carnegie, you are now the richest man in the world."

It was at this point in his life that Carnegie turned reflective about the unheard-of size of his fortune. He adopted the credo that "to die wealthy is to die disgraced" and set his course on giving away his wealth for the betterment of society. His beneficiaries were innumerable. He established the Carnegie Corporation of New York with a $125,000,000 endowment. The purpose of this fund was to award educational grants for research, and since its formation in 1911, the fund has awarded more than $400,000,000 in awards. A lover of books and a lifelong believer in the power of an enlightened mind, he personally oversaw the construction of 2,500 public libraries across the globe. He built Carnegie Hall in New York City, one of the premier concert halls in the world. He supplied 8,000 organs for churches nationwide, for free! He gave $10,000,000 to establish a Scottish University Trust in honor of his homeland, where he built Skibo Castle, his second home. One of his most recognizable legacies is the Carnegie Hero Fund, which has awarded millions of dollars to ordinary citizens who have performed extraordinary acts of bravery.

Dedicating oneself to the dispersal of a fortune amounting to hundreds of millions of dollars was a daunting task. But Carnegie was a man inspired to succeed and, except for personal bequests and family obligations, he died on August 11, 1919, having given almost all of it away!

Andrew Carnegie is buried in Sleepy Hollow Cemetery, Sleepy Hollow, New York.

Although this worldly and wealthy legend could have afforded the most extravagant mausoleum ever built, Carnegie rests beneath a simple, rugged Celtic cross made out of stones taken from his Scottish home. In this "Cemetery of Millionaires" (Rockefellers, Chryslers, etc.), the richest man of them all is buried with none of the trappings that hinted of his storied wealth.

Author's note: Carnegie libraries still stand throughout the land. Many libraries are denoted as Carnegie gifts and highlighted as local historic landmarks. Carnegie was called "The Patron Saint of Libraries," and his largess was not exclusive to the United States. He built 1,681 public libraries in America, 660 in the United Kingdom, 125 in Canada, and dozens more around the world. He even built one in Fiji!

You could take Andrew Carnegie's word straight to the bank. As a young man, he vowed to his mother that he would never marry while she was alive. His mother finally died when he was fifty-one; he married at fifty-two and had his first and only child at age sixty-two!

In 1996, the village of North Tarrytown officially changed its name to the more bumper sticker friendly Sleepy Hollow, New York. It is located in the deep Hudson River Valley, near the eastern terminus of the Tappan Zee Bridge. Sleepy Hollow Cemetery is located at 540 N. Broadway (914-631-0081). It is open to the public every day and offers miles of trickling creeks, gravel footpaths, and rustic bridges for the visitor to explore. Without question, it is one of the most historic and beautiful cemeteries in the state. A free map can be obtained at the front gate that will send you off on several hours' worth of exploring.

The graves of the mighty stand shoulder to shoulder along the bucolic boulevards: Thomas Watson, Sr., founder of IBM; automaker Walter Chrysler; labor leader Samuel Gompers; artist Jasper Cropsey; radio and television pioneer "Major" Bowes; fashion doyenne Elizabeth Arden; oil tycoon William Rockefeller; Carnegie; and many others. William Rockefeller is the only "Rocky" buried here, although his enormous mausoleum (the largest in the cemetery) stands alongside a black wrought-iron fence that marks the start of Kykuit, the Rockefeller family estate at Pocantico Hills. Among the more curious buried here are Ann Trow Lohman ("The Wickedest Woman in New York") and writer Washington Irving. Lohman and William Rockefeller are also included in this book. Irving's grave is the most visited site of them all, and helpful road signs will point you easily to his final resting place. He was one of the earliest trustees of the cemetery. Adjacent to the graveyard is the Old Dutch Church, built in 1685. It is open to the public, and it is wonderful. Though not officially connected with the cemetery, it shares a common, natural boundary. The church and its surrounds are the setting for Irving's classic *The Legend of Sleepy Hollow*.

ANNA MARY ROBERTSON

"Grandma Moses"

What a life she had!

Born before the Civil War and living through both World Wars, Anna Robertson preferred to look at life on the brighter side. Born in poverty, she only had a few short months of schooling before her father pulled her out and instructed her on the "womanly arts" of cooking, sewing, candle making, and gardening. She was raised in a family of ten children, and at age twenty-seven, she married Thomas Salmon Moses, with whom she then had her own ten children (only five survived infancy). She first took up painting at the age of seventy after arthritis prohibited her from making and selling needlework. By this age, she was known to all as Grandma Moses.

She lived for more than a half-century in the area around Eagle's Bridge/Hoosick Falls, New York. The legend of her fame began in 1939 when she placed several of her paintings in a drug store window on Main Street of Hoosick Falls. There they languished for years. She had given many of her pieces to friends before this. One day, an art collector from New York City happened by the window and saw her paintings. His name was Louis Caldor. He asked how much the paintings cost and if there were more of them. The clerk told Caldor that Moses had ten more paintings out at her farm, and the collector headed out to see her. One story reports that upon hearing of this, Grandma Moses realized that she really only had nine paintings available. She cut the largest one in half to make ten!

Caldor took all of her artwork to New York and exhibited three pieces at the famed Museum of Modern Art in a show called "Contemporary, Unknown Painters." An immediate critical success, within one year Moses was mounting a one-woman show at Galerie St. Etienne in Manhattan, and art fans were clamoring for her work. She was seventy-nine years old at the time.

Grandma Moses produced more than 2,000 paintings during her career, most of them on crude masonite board, using her typical primitive style of starting the painting out at the top with the sky, then the trees and mountains, then the buildings and the people and animals. She only painted what she called "old timey things" from her rural past—holiday meals, Christmas in New England, barn raisings, pumpkin patches, apple pickers, and more. In 1945, Hallmark Cards purchased the rights to reproduce her paintings on greeting cards and sold six million of them in the first year.

Moses defined the word *prolific*. Incredibly, of the 2,000 paintings she produced in her lifetime, more than 250 of them were done *after* she reached her 100th birthday!

Near the end of her life, in 1955 at age ninety-six, she was a guest on the Edward R. Murrow interview show *See It Now*. She charmed the nation. When Murrow asked her what uniquely qualified her to be an artist, she gave a crinkly wry smile, shoved a piece of paper in front of him, and said, "Here. Draw a tree. Anybody can paint!"

Upon her death on December 13, 1961, at the age of 101, President John F. Kennedy called her "our national treasure." She is buried with her husband in Upper Maple Grove Cemetery in Hoosick Falls, just a dusty walk down the dirt road from the drug store window where it all started for her in 1939.

Author's note: Hoosick Falls, population six thousand, is located thirty-three miles east of Albany. Take Route 7 to Hoosick and go north four miles on Route 22 to Hoosick Falls. The cemetery is located on this road (known locally as Main Street). This area is one of the most beautiful the Empire State has to offer, and every bend in the road seems to bring to the visitor a page right out of a Grandma Moses calendar—dairy herds lazing about in green pastures, bright red barns with gaily colored clothes flapping on the clothesline, kids playing in the front yards, and quaint New England towns and homes seemingly stopped in time. A walking tour of Main Street will reveal plaques telling you of the historic spots in Grandma Moses's life around town (such as the drug store where she was first discovered). Signs at the cemetery will point you to her burial site. Her large stone reads, "Anna Mary Robertson. GRANDMA MOSES. Her primitive paintings captured the spirit and preserved the scene of a vanishing countryside."

A visitor to this area would be well-advised to make the short (twenty-minute) trip across the Vermont border to Bennington. This picture-postcard New England community is home to the acclaimed Bennington Museum, a rural showplace that features the largest collection of Moses's paintings in the world. Also, check out the Grandma Moses Schoolhouse, where she originally attended school (briefly) in Eagle's Bridge. It was moved to the museum in 1972. Inside, visitors can watch the historic original tape of the famous Edward R. Murrow interview with her. For information about the museum, call 802-447-1571.

HELEN HAYES

"First Lady of the American Theater"

The role of Queen Victoria was exhausting. On stage for nearly three hours, this featured role required the actress to age more than fifty years. The costumes were elaborate, heavy, and very hot. A skullcap was pulled tight over the head of the performer to afford easy hairstyle changes. Volumes of lines and staging marks had to be memorized.

The role of Ada Quonsett was a quirky one. Not just any "character actress" could pull it off. In a drama about life and death and terror, Ada was a spunky, iron-willed shyster whose role in saving lives was all-important. The main cast consisted of some of Hollywood's most famous and reliable actors: Dean Martin, Burt Lancaster, Maureen Stapleton, Van Heflin, George Kennedy, Jean Seberg, and Lloyd Nolan. The role of Ada Quonsett was eighth-billed but was key to the development of the drama. Yes, few actresses could pull off this sensitive assignment, and the studio knew that the whole picture could perhaps hang in the balance of this casting call.

Regal Queen Victoria and sprightly Ada Quonsett. Roles so far apart and yet, in a strange way, so similar. Both characters required a performer who could "lose" herself to the role. Both required an actress who could make the part more than believable. Both roles required an artist who could command every scene she was in. There was only one actress to fit the bill, Helen Hayes, "The First Lady of the American Theater."

Hayes starred as Queen Victoria in *Victoria Regina* on Broadway early on in her seventy-five-year career. As the greatest star of the Great White Way, she owned Manhattan. Critics called her Queen Victoria "definitive" and "a masterpiece."

Forty years later, she was tapped again to deliver. This time in the multimillion dollar Universal Pictures film *Airport*. Now herself in her seventies, Hayes scored big with the audiences as Ada Quonsett and took home the Oscar that year for Best Supporting Actress. *Airport* was one of the top three pictures of the year.

Helen Hayes was a remarkable actress. Starting at the age of eight, she was on Broadway for almost the entire twentieth century. Her mother, an acting "wannabe," drove young Helen (then known as Helen Hayes Brown) to New York City where Lew Fields discovered the young girl's talents and starred her in successive hits. Before she was ten, her name was star-billed on the brightest marquees of Broadway.

Talkies were the novelty in Hollywood, and her migration west was inevitable. Along the way, she married the brilliant playwright and novelist Charles MacArthur. MacArthur, then on the verge of major success himself, was a dark-haired man-about-town who absolutely swept Helen off her feet. Their courtship was the stuff of Hollywood legends. The story is told that they met at a cocktail party in New York. Hayes asked MacArthur if he would get her some peanuts from the bar. When he returned, he took her open hand and slowly poured out a stream of peanuts into it. Hayes gazed up at the young playwright and flirted, "I wish these were emeralds." Two years later, after MacArthur's *The Front Page* became the biggest hit on Broadway, she once again asked him to get her some nuts. When he returned after a short while, he took her opened palm and poured a stream of priceless emeralds into it. Hayes looked up at her then-husband and whispered, "I wish these were peanuts."

In contrast to her regal title of "First Lady," Hayes was known as Helen to all who met her. Her greatest joy came from her home and rose gardens at the mansion she owned in Nyack, New York, "Pretty Penny." It was a large, seven-bedroom Victorian mansion set high on a bluff overlooking the Hudson River. This house was her oasis from a life of celebrity and publicity. Her passion for roses resulted in one of the most extensive and acclaimed rose gardens in New York. In fact, a "Helen Hayes Rose" was named in her honor.

From Broadway to Hollywood, Helen Hayes was one of a kind. She won an Oscar for her very first film (*The Sin of Madalon Claudet*) in 1931 and holds the record for the longest span of time between Academy Awards (forty years, 1931-1971). She won Emmys for her television work, Tonys for her work on Broadway, and too many honors, accolades, and public opinion awards to name. She has a Broadway theater named after her in New York.

On stage, Helen Hayes was so formidable a talent that she was recast repeatedly in some of the theater's most challenging roles, despite her advancement in age. For example, she starred in Thornton Wilder's *The Skin of Our Teeth* twice, in 1955 and in 1961. And she starred in Tennessee Williams' masterpiece *The Glass Menagerie* three times: 1948, 1956, and 1961.

Beloved by all Americans, she won virtually every honor imaginable, from the Kennedy Center Honors in 1981 to the Presidential Medal of Freedom in 1986. Her golden years were spent reaping the rewards of a rich and *en*riched life. In her final three years, she spent her time at Pretty Penny reflecting on her life's ups and downs, and there were some very serious downs. Her husband eventually drank himself to death, and her only natural child, daughter Mary, died of polio at nineteen. She recalled it all in her 1990 best-selling autobiography *My Life in Three Acts*.

Hayes died on St. Patrick's Day, 1993, at the age of ninety-two. Her funeral, in Nyack, was officiated by John Cardinal O'Connor of New York. Throngs of townspeople came to pay their last respects to Helen at St. Anne's Roman Catholic Church on Jefferson Street. They remembered the "little old lady" who would stand along Nyack's Main Street waving a tiny American flag during the Fourth of July parade, or the lady who would wait in line just like everybody else to get the *TV Guide* at the local grocery store. Everybody, it seemed, had a wonderful memory of her in this small town. And all were pleased that she had come back to Nyack to rest eternally.

Helen Hayes is buried in Oak Hill Cemetery, Nyack, New York.

Author's note: You will find the cemetery entrance just across the street from Nyack Hospital. To get to Hayes's grave (the MacArthur family plot), enter through the main gate and follow the road to the top of the hill. She is buried with her husband and daughter in the Grand View Lawn Section, near the center, in Lot #51. From Helen Hayes's grave, a visitor has a breathtaking view of the panoramic Hudson River Valley below, as well as the Tappan Zee Bridge. Nyack is located at the western entrance to the bridge. Pretty Penny was bought in recent years by talk-show host Rosie O'Donnell. Hayes's adopted son, James MacArthur, is remembered for his co-starring role as "Danno" in the long-running police drama *Hawaii 5-0.*

It is curious to note that actress Helen Hayes and singer Kate Smith were girlhood friends in Washington, D.C. From that early beginning, both young ladies would go on to become worldwide celebrities, Helen as "First Lady of the Theater" and Kate as the "First Lady of Radio." It is also remarkable that, similarly, these two legendary Americans would be buried in tiny Upstate New York towns that they called home for decades, Nyack and Lake Placid. (Smith is also included in this book.)

E. Z. C. JUDSON

"Ned Buntline: King of the Dime Novel"

Ned Buntline was a bit of a fraud.

Born Edward Zane Carroll Judson in rural Stamford, New York, his life was filled with unverifiable tales of daring, his military career was undistinguished (yet he called himself "Colonel"), and his success as a writer hinged on the embroidered tales of a glorified buffalo hunter. Despite all this (or perhaps because of it), Ned Buntline (EZC Judson) was one of the most famous and colorful literary figures of the "Old West."

One remarkable event, that is verified, certainly must place his name in the forefront of frontier legends. In March of 1848, he killed Robert Porterfield, with whose wife Judson was having an affair in Tennessee. At his murder trial, the late Porterfield's brother opened fire on him, and Judson flung himself out of the courthouse window and escaped. Soon he was recaptured, jailed, and sentenced to death. Unbelievably, at the time of his execution, the hangman's noose *broke* when the trap door swung open, and Judson, his neck still intact, was (by law) a free man!

Later, in New York City, he founded a popular scandal sheet, *Ned Buntline's Own*, which was the most successful of its kind anywhere. He was convicted of starting a riot in the city (the famous Astor Place Riot) on May 10, 1849, and this time served a year in prison. In 1852, he again was indicted on charges of causing another riot, this time on election day in St. Louis, but escaped prosecution by jumping bail. Eventually he relieved himself of all legal entanglements and concentrated on his popular writings. Through skillfully placed news reports of his antics and through the power of his own prose (in which he usually was the prototype of his fictional heroes), Judson became a "cause celebre" and a tremendously popular personality.

Using the pseudonym of Ned Buntline, he wrote over four hundred inexpensive adventure books (hence the "dime novel"). Each was more eagerly anticipated than the last by his reading public. In 1869, he met a twenty-three-year-old buffalo hunter named William F. Cody. Christening him "Buffalo Bill," Judson brought his daring tales of life on the frontier to the public through several books and articles featuring the intriguing plainsman. By the time he wrote the stage play, *Scouts of the Prairie*, starring Cody, each man's public stature was at its zenith.

Judson married four times and was chased by ex-wives most of the last decades of his life. In 1871, at last a wealthy man, he retired to his magnificent mansion, "Eagle's Nest," in Stamford. There he continued to write until his death on July 16, 1886, at the age of sixty-four. In these twilight years, Col. Judson was a familiar sight in the upper circles of Catskill society. With his drooping white walrus mustache and his bemedaled vest, he was always a welcome and sought-after dinner guest. Eagle's Nest was the scene of many sparkling galas attended by the literati of the region, all eager to hear once again the stories of "Ned Buntline" and Buffalo Bill and the glory days of the *real* Old West.

Author's note: Judson is buried in Stamford Rural Cemetery, located off Route 23 at the very southern entrance to the village of Stamford (Delaware County). Drive up Cemetery Road five hundred feet, and the actual cemetery entrance is on your right. Drive in as far as the dirt road travels until it bends to the left. You'll see, straight ahead, the tall red-brown obelisk bearing the name E. Z. C. Judson.

Eagle's Nest is still a Stamford, New York, landmark. It is located off Main Street on Buntline Road, at the base of towering Mt. Utsayantha, and any resident can point you the way. Sorry, it is not open to the public and is indeed in need of great repair. The Stamford Public Library on Main Street offers a wealth of reading material about Buntline, Eagle's Nest, and old Stamford life.

Outside the cemetery, make a right and head up the hill. A drive to the top of Mt. Utsayantha offers the visitor one of the most spectacular views of the upper Catskill region (it is a seasonal road). The tall fire tower on the top of the mountain was restored in 2005 and opened to the public (the climb is not for the faint of heart, but the view is worth it). Built in 1934, it is one of the last of the famous Catskill Mountain fire towers still in use. A parking lot and picnic area can also be found there. On a clear day, "you can see forever."

Henry Wells
and William Fargo _____

"The Wells Fargo Company"

The image is vivid: a dashing stagecoach hurtling along at breakneck speed barely outdistancing a pistol-blasting band of undesirables ... the frightened passengers crouching low for protection ... the gold-laden strongbox bouncing wildly on the roof ... the driver straining and whipping and shouting his steeds onward ... and the familiar, reassuring name emblazoned in red across the side of the carriage, "WELLS FARGO." Such was the stuff that legends were made of!

Henry Wells established a delivery route between Albany and Buffalo in 1843. He worked as a messenger between these two cities, often making the trip himself no fewer than five times a week (no small feat when you consider that each trip combined the use of six different railroads and two stage lines). He charged six cents per letter carried and made a pretty good living. Seeking to increase his area of service, he joined William Fargo in establishing Wells and Company, which incorporated the use of ships and barges so as to include the booming Great Lakes region around Chicago and Detroit. It was an immediate success, and in 1850, they merged all of their many routes together and formed the largest express company in the country, the American Express Company. They also continued to grow the business that still bears their names today and expanded their delivery routes from the East Coast to the West Coast, and from California all the way up to the gold coast of the Pacific Northwest.

Henry Wells was the president of the firm, Fargo the secretary. As like-minded and as business-wise as both men were, two more different personalities you would never find. Henry Wells was a shy, meek number-cruncher who was plagued with a stammering speech impediment all of his life. He was contemplative and enjoyed his privacy and such refined amusements as travel and the opera. Fargo, on the other hand, was an outgoing, backslapping, no-nonsense achiever who was the "engine" behind the company's expansion and financial success.

Both men lived extraordinary lives after they left the business arena, seeking compatible endeavors in which to enjoy their retirement and spend their hard-earned fortunes. Wells retired from American Express and Wells Fargo Company and moved to tiny Aurora, New York. There on the shores of beautiful Cayuga Lake, he became a bank president and a college founder (Wells College). He also dedicated a large portion of his great wealth to funding speech therapy schools around the country. Fargo, the extrovert of the two, went back to his home base of Buffalo and ran for public office. A widely popular figure, he served as that city's mayor during the Civil War, from 1862 to 1866.

Both men are buried in their chosen hometowns and are honored in these communities for their separate achievements.

Author's note: Henry Wells is buried in the old cemetery off Main Street in Aurora, which is located just west of the city of Auburn along NYS Route 90, midway up the eastern shore of Cayuga

Lake. Exit Main Street at Cherry Avenue (across from the town post office) and you will soon see Oak Glen Cemetery on your right. Enter and go straight back about halfway through the cemetery. Wells's tall, pointy obelisk is in the center and is unmistakable. Tiny, forgotten Aurora Oak Glen Cemetery has no office or personnel. Fittingly, you will pass Wells College on your way to this cemetery. Wells College is a historic institution having established the second baccalaureate degree for women in America. It made news recently when it announced it was allowing men to enroll for the first time in an effort to stem the flow of red ink amounting to a debt growing at more than $5,000,000 per year. Despite a few noisy protestations from alumni and benefactors, Wells College went co-ed for the first time in its 136-year history in 2005. For information regarding Wells College, call 315-364-3266.

William Fargo is buried in famous Forest Lawn Cemetery in Buffalo, New York. Forest Lawn Cemetery is one of the largest and most beautiful cemeteries in the whole Upstate region. There is much to see at Forest Lawn and many notable "residents" to observe. It is imperative that you stop at the main gate, where friendly personnel will give you a highlighted map of the cemetery, directing you to the gravesites of William Fargo, President Millard Fillmore (included in this book), Seneca Chief Red Jacket, and others. An amazing feature is the Blocher Memorial. It is the cemetery's "centerpiece" gravesite. An incredible sixty-ton monument holds the likenesses of the four deceased family members in varying states of repose behind glass panels. The exactness of the carvings is astonishing. Thousands come from all around the nation to stand awestruck at this eerie and stunning tomb. Other famous residents of this park-like cemetery include Sarah Hinson, who created Flag Day; America Pinckney

Williams, the great-granddaughter of Martha Washington; Margaret St. John, the "Heroine of Buffalo," who refused to move her nine children when the British threatened to burn Buffalo to the ground in 1813 (they did, but spared her house); Willis Carrier, the "Father of Air Conditioning"; Frederick Cook, the first claimant to the discovery of the North Pole; Dorothy Berlin, first wife of songwriter Irving Berlin; John Frank Hoover, who caught John Wilkes Booth; Louise Bethune, America's first female architect; and many others. Forest Lawn Cemetery, 1411 Delaware Avenue, Buffalo, New York, can be reached at 716-885-1600. The vast cemetery is a popular strolling place for many walkers each summer weekend.

FREDERICK DOUGLASS

"Emancipation's Voice"

With his fierce, leonine look, his glowering eyes, his impeccably tailored clothes, and his "from Hell and back" thundering voice, Frederick Douglass was considered by many to be the most important African-American figure of the entire nineteenth century. Born into slavery, he rose to the highest pinnacles of fame and notoriety as the voice of the anti-slavery movement in America.

Douglass was living in bondage in the city of Baltimore when he decided it was time for him to join his brothers in the North in their fight against slavery. Maryland, at that time, required every black man to carry identification papers describing him accurately and stating his situation (free or owned). Douglass disguised himself as a sailor and endured a frightening twenty-four-hour flight to freedom to New York City. He would later recall that there were many times along that harrowing journey that he knew he had been recognized, but friends had remained silent and let him pass. He felt as if "God had let him escape from a den of hungry lions."

Douglass was a publisher of note. He authored the two most important anti-slavery journals of the day, *North Star* and *The Frederick Douglass Paper*, which brought all of the latest abolition news to the free and slave alike. His life did hold a certain degree of mystery to it. A few contradictions caused him great concern. A passionate fighter for the freeing of slaves, Douglass refused to support John Brown's raid on Harper's Ferry and in fact denounced it. As the son of a black mother and a white father, his detractors called him a fraud as a civil-rights spokesman. In 1845, he authored *The Narrative Life of Frederick Douglass: American Slave* to dispel any suspicions. After the publication of this work, and on the heels of the John Brown fiasco, he traveled to Europe, where he was welcomed as a great champion of emancipation. (It was here, a year later, that friends purchased his permanent freedom for 150 British pounds.)

Douglass was a confidant of several U.S. presidents, and Grant appointed him to the position of Marshal of Washington, then Assistant Secretary in Santo Domingo, then General Consul in Haiti. He wrote two more well-received books, *My Bondage* (1855) and *The Life and Times of Frederick Douglass* (1881).

A powerful and important personality to the end of his life, his passing on February 20, 1895, was mourned on a national scale. He was buried with much pomp at famous Mt. Hope Cemetery, in Rochester, New York.

Author's note: Mt. Hope Cemetery in Rochester is one of the largest and most famous in Upstate New York. After entering the cemetery off Mount Hope Avenue, make your first right on Fifth Avenue (inside the cemetery). Go through the second intersection and stop. In the middle of the section on your right, near to and overlooking the street, is the giant stone slab with the black metal letters reading "FREDERICK DOUGLASS 1817-1895." Many recognizable names, including Susan B. Anthony (see her entry in this book), can be found among the nearly 450,000 graves. The cemetery (716-473-2755) is at 719 Mount Hope Avenue, Rochester, New York.

As one of our history's most famous Black Americans, Douglass has been honored in a variety of ways, from being featured on a U.S. postage stamp to having a ship named after him. Two sites of national importance should be mentioned. The Frederick Douglass Museum and Cultural Center is currently being organized at 25 E. Main Street in downtown Rochester, New York, Douglass's hometown. The 35,000-square-foot Tallman Building, a five-story landmark, will eventually be the site of this educational and historical center in Douglass's name. It was at this address that he published his two anti-slavery journals, and this building was also a major stop on the Underground Railroad. For events and information, call 715-546-3960. The Frederick Douglass National Historic Site in Washington, D.C. was his home from 1877 to 1895. "Cedar Hill" sits high atop a small hill in the Anacostia section of our nation's capital, at 1411 W Street SE (near W Street and 15th Street). For events, call 202-426-5961. This beautifully restored home was made a national historic site in 1988. A free seventeen-minute film on Douglass's life is shown frequently at the visitors center. A small fee is charged for a tour of the home and grounds. Of interest is a large painting in the center hallway of Cedar Hill. It depicts the fateful charge on Fort Wagner by the black soldiers of the 54th Massachusetts Regiment during the Civil War (a battle memorialized in the Denzel Washington film *Glory*). Douglass's two sons, Charles and Lewis, were members of the 54th and took part in that attack.

JAMES FENIMORE COOPER

"Leatherstocking Tales"

James Fenimore Cooper has been called America's first popular writer. He was born the eleventh of twelve children in a town built by his father and named for his family (Cooperstown, New York). In 1821, he found sudden fame with the publication of only his second novel, *The Spy*. His legacy in the annals of early American literature is without question. His exciting tales of Indians and frontiersmen were huge bestsellers at the time and are still, almost two centuries later, required reading for many young high school students. *The Deerslayer*, *The Last of the Mohicans*, *The Pathfinder*, and *The Pioneers* are as vivid today as when they were first written. Together the books comprise Cooper's epic Leatherstocking Tales. Many movies have been made of his books over the years, particularly *The Last of the Mohicans*, which has had several Hollywood treatments.

A man raised in the gentry, Cooper lived the last several years of his life at his family mansion in Cooperstown and died on September 14, 1851. He is buried at Christ Church in Cooperstown, a church built by his father,

Judge William Cooper, in 1810. So great was his fame that at his funeral, eulogies were offered by some of America's most famous personalities: Washington Irving, Daniel Webster, and William Cullen Bryant.

Author's note: While there is certainly no question that James Fenimore Cooper was a towering figure in American literature, there can also be no question that perhaps one of his greatest legacies is in fact the very town that bears his name. Historical markers around the lake and throughout the village tell of the events of Cooper's novels. A massive statue of Cooper, sitting pensively looking out over the lake, is a much-photographed place. The word *Cooper* can be found on nearly every business or building.

Cooperstown was founded by his father, who cleared the forest around Lake Otsego at the turn of the nineteenth century. Christ Church, the Cooper "family" church, is one of the most beautiful little churches in all of Upstate New York. Tiny in scope, there is an aura of grandeur inside. Brilliant original stained-glass windows (two by Tiffany), ornate hand-carved woodwork, and historic altarpieces make it a true treasure. The nave and the tower are original parts of the church. In 1840, stone additions were erected under the supervision of James Fenimore Cooper himself. Having just returned from Europe, he oversaw the transformation of the interior of *his* church from Romanesque to the more Gothic design then all the rage in Europe. The church sits just a block south of Cooperstown's Main Street, near the site of Otsego Hall, the Cooper mansion (now gone).

The graveyard next to Christ Church is filled with two hundred years' worth of Cooper history. James's gravestone notes only his birth and death dates. Judge Cooper is buried nearby. Some believe the judge was killed in a duel in 1809 in Albany; others say he was murdered by an angry political opponent while exiting an Albany tavern. Whatever the case, mystery still shrouds the death of the judge. Among the other old graves here, a stroll up and down the well-manicured rows will illustrate some graves as old as 1792. Notice one marked, "Joe Tom, slave." Another is that of Joe Tom's daughter who died at the age of one hundred. In the Cooper section, family veterans are represented from virtually every war America ever fought in. The most recent Cooper burials are less than thirty years old, making this one of the oldest known *active* family cemeteries in the state.

The village of Cooperstown, almost in the geographical center of New York, is filled with historic homes, landmarks, and museums. A weekend visit is needed to do this community justice (www. CooperstownWalks.com). From the famous statue of the Indian scout sculpted by John Quincy Adams Ward in the beautiful Lakefront Park to Cooper's ancestral home, Fenimore House (now the home of the New York State Historical Association), there is much to see and learn and explore in Cooper Country. For information about revolving exhibits at the Fenimore House, go to www.nysha.org.

A word to the wise: All Cooperphiles exploring this community and Cooper's life would be well advised to schedule a visit in the spring or fall. Not only are the hills around Lake Otsego (which Cooper called "The Glimmerglass") a crazy quilt of blazing autumn colors, but the crowds are also thinner. The National Baseball Hall of Fame on Main Street, Cooperstown draws more than a *quarter of a million visitors yearly* to this community of only 2,500!

BEGORDIUS HATCH

"The Strongest Man in Washington's Army"

The history of the Hudson Valley is filled with tales of strange happenings and colorful people. Some are true, and some are fable. Generations have been dazzled by tales of everything from a headless horseman to a gent who slept for twenty years. One legend that *is* fact is the story of Begordius Hatch. He was raised in the upper Hudson Valley near New Lebanon and rests there now in a forgotten and overgrown cemetery. He fathered thirteen children, and Hatch descendents still flourish along the river valley. They called him "The Strongest Man in Washington's Army," and his story is amazing.

Orphaned at four, Hatch was raised by a farmer until he was sixteen. It was at this age that he ran away from home to join up with George Washington's army at the Battle of Boston Heights. The general was intrigued by this towering, powerfully built recruit and signed Hatch on as his personal bodyguard. Hatch showed his gratitude to Washington with unswerving loyalty, and in fact was one of only a handful of men to serve in each of Washington's campaigns.

During the years that Hatch was in the army, there were long periods of inactivity between hostilities. During this peaceful time, the soldiers would keep fit by boxing, wrestling, and holding weight-lifting contests. No one dared challenge Hatch, though. Washington would prod the gentle giant into putting on amazing shows of strength for the troops. Often, Hatch would hoist a cast-iron cannon onto his massive shoulders and parade it around in front of the astonished men. Washington took great pleasure in showing Hatch off, but he was also sincerely grateful to his bodyguard for getting him through the war without a scratch.

At the close of the war, General Washington expressed his great thanks to Hatch and dismissed him. Hatch shyly smiled and simply turned around and walked away. *All the way!* In fact, he didn't stop walking until he was home with his family, a trek of over *125 miles!*

At home in New Lebanon, the man who was known as one of the world's strongest humans took up farming and began to raise a large family. The nearby Indians respected his great strength and left him and his farm in peace. A gentle man of deep compassion, Hatch was a personable fellow with a cheery disposition. He was always ready to help his neighbors bring in the harvest or raise up a barn (and, because of his might, he was asked to do both often).

One story that still makes the rounds around the valley is of the time, in 1836, that Hatch was challenged by his neighbors. He was then seventy-five years old and in the last year of his life. A band of friends had invited him to a barn-raising. They schemed a joke on Hatch that would "prove" to them his fabled strength. They positioned him in the middle of a large beam and put six farmhands on each side of him. At the signal, the farmhands would feign lifting and leave all the work to Hatch. At the command of "heave," the twelve stood limply by the side as the mighty Begordius Hatch lifted the giant beam alone, slowly walked to the ladder, climbed to the roof, and placed it where it belonged. He then came down the ladder, looked up at the amazed farmhands, and gave them a sly wink of the eye. He then strode off to his home. The crowd broke into applause.

Hatch died on May 24, 1836, and is buried in West Hill Cemetery, New Lebanon, New York.

Author's note: New Lebanon is a beautiful town with much history. Tucked along the New England border just inside the New York line, it is located twenty-five miles southeast of Albany amidst the gentle foothills of the Taconic Range. This is Shaker country, and there are many historic sites to see for the traveler with a little time on his hands.

To get to West Hill Cemetery, travel along Upper West Street from New Lebanon to four miles past the town line sign. The cemetery is on the right. It is small and very overgrown (or was on the day I was there). Walk all the way to the very rear of the cemetery and you will find Hatch's gravestone. Look for the "handshake," a chiseled depiction of two hands shaking, on his marker (which reads: "A life how useful to his country led, how loved when living, how revered now dead"). A small American flag usually flies nearby. New York State politician Samuel J. Tilden was perhaps the most famous resident of New Lebanon. His story is also told in this book.

ANN LEE

"The Word"

Ann Lee dropped out of school in her native England at a very young age and went to work. The work was often menial yet productive (she never learned to read or write). She often toiled as a house cleaner or as some other domestic servant. An unusual child in many ways, she was a hard worker who had few social interests. In 1762, she married a local blacksmith named Abraham Standerin and bore him four children in quick succession. Each birth was a painful and difficult ordeal for Ann, and each of her four children died in infancy. This experience was the catalyst that transformed a quiet and private young woman into the well-known and forceful "Mother Ann," who many would believe was the embodiment of the second coming of Christ.

Lee joined a cultish group of religious zealots called the Shakers shortly after the death of her last child. The Shakers (so called because of the wildly exotic gyrations they performed in their "exorcism" dances) had a tiny, yet loyal, following in England. Ann, convinced that sexual intercourse had been the devil's tool in her own life, was an enthusiastic convert to the Shakers and quickly became one of their leaders. In 1770, she was imprisoned for "acts against the Sabbath" and became a martyr to her followers. When she emerged from prison, she announced that she had had a vision in her jail cell and that this vision had convinced her that all of mankind's ills were brought on by the sex act. The vision, she went on, told her that she, Ann, was the female mentioned in the Bible in Revelation 12 (a passage which described a "woman of Grace"). Upon her release, she was hailed as being one "close to God" and was elevated into the hierarchy of the Shaker movement.

In 1774, a second vision directed her to go to America to start a Shaker community. She, her husband, and a small cadre of supporters came to an area of Upstate New York near Albany (around the city of Watervliet) and began recruiting new disciples.

Her program of absolute celibacy was in stark contrast to her more sensible beliefs in communal living. The theory that shared tasks made shared harmony appealed to many in the audiences at her meetings, and soon a full-fledged Shaker community was established in 1776. Taking the name "Mother Ann" (or the more messianic "The Word"), Lee traveled across New England preaching complete and total celibacy as the way to a more pure and peaceful existence. In many small towns and villages she visited, this tiny woman with the shocking message was met with harassment and violence. On several occasions, she was stoned by angry mobs. Still she persevered and was successful in establishing eleven Shaker communities in the region.

Lee's demeanor was kindly and gentle, with a loving quality about her. Yet she exhibited steely determination when it came to her principles and beliefs. She was nobody's fool and, over time, became isolated from those who found her theories and tenets extreme. The years of public persecution and ridicule eventually began to exact a terrible toll on her health. She had become the favorite target for detractors in ever-growing numbers and was imprisoned repeatedly. In 1780, she was famously jailed for "high treason" for preaching non-violence and pacifism during the Revolutionary War.

Those disciples in her service stayed steadfast throughout. They described her as a God-like messiah whose theories on hard work, love, celibacy, and honesty made her an iconic leader. Still she paid an enormous price for her beliefs, and, with her health in a dramatic spiral, she passed away on September 8, 1784, at only the age of forty-eight. "The Word" is buried in the Old Shaker Cemetery in Albany.

Author's note: The Shaker Burial Ground is actually on the grounds of the Shaker Heritage Site. The cemetery is on Airline Road just three blocks south of Albany International Airport. At Heritage Park, you will find the Shaker Society Museum and Gift Shop and other original Shaker outbuildings. A historical marker denotes the 1916 Shaker Church Family Barn and the location of "America's First Shaker Settlement." The Shaker cemetery features hundreds of identical grave markers, each bearing the first name of the deceased, the year of his or her death, and the age at death. In the center of these many headstones stands one that is just like all of the others, except that it is four inches taller. This is the grave of Mother Ann Lee.

WILLIAM ROCKEFELLER

"The Millionaire Salesman of Standard Oil"

It is interesting to note that in a state so indelibly imprinted with the name "ROCKEFELLER" the only gravesite accessible to the public of a member of New York's premier family is that of little-known William Rockefeller. Although it was his lot to stand in the shadow of his legendary brother, John D., most of his life, William was able to carve out a profitable piece of the Rockefeller-pie that eventually became known as Standard Oil.

While the Rockefeller brothers shared many of the same attributes, it was William's success as a salesman that gained him his own fortune. John D. and William started Standard Oil from scratch and led it to its position as the country's leading source of oil products. William was the salesman part of the team and was extremely successful in introducing their oil to the far-flung growing markets around the world. He invested in copper, railroads, mines, and banks. His participation in a copper investment was nearly his undoing, however. With the government investigating charges that he "rigged the market" and that he caused the failure of a major bank, he was spared the agony and public humiliation of an official public inquiry only because his health turned conveniently bad. A judge ruled him unfit to stand trial, and the charges were ultimately dismissed. (In all fairness, it was rumored that he was suffering from throat cancer for years and truly was in failing health at the time of the controversy.) A second scar on the Rockefeller image was the famous Ludlow Massacre at a family-owned mine in Colorado. It took millions of dollars and many years to clean up what many perceived as a major public relations disaster.

In the image of his more famous brother, William Rockefeller was a magnanimous philanthropist. While always preferring to remain anonymous, many of his huge contributions were well noted in the press. For one cause alone, The United States War Relief Fund (WW I), he wrote a personal check for one million dollars.

He worked steadily into his eighties and in fact was walking to work in the rain (on a Saturday, no less!) on June 17, 1922, when he caught a severe cold. In a week he was dead.

One of the only major Rockefellers of his era not to be buried at the family estate of "Pocantico Hills," William is buried in adjoining Sleepy Hollow Cemetery, Sleepy Hollow, New York.

Author's note: His tomb at Sleepy Hollow Cemetery is the most expensive and grand of any of the thousands there. Enter the main gate of the cemetery off Broadway (Route 9) and make your first major left turn on Central Avenue (inside the cemetery). Then make a quick right on Vernon Avenue and stop. Walk a few short steps to the north. A massive, thirty-two-ton columned Greek mausoleum, it simply cannot be missed. Rockefeller personally supervised the construction of his own tomb, and the final tab for the granite and marble grave was well over $250,000. On one side of the tomb, the name WILLIAM ROCKEFELLER is chiseled in prominent letters nearly two feet tall. On the other side reads this inscription: "Thou hast made us for thyself, and our heart shall never rest until at last it rests in Thee." He left an estate, which would make any Rockefeller proud, of $150,000,000. Among the other industrial giants buried in Sleepy Hollow Cemetery is Walter Chrysler, the automaker. His towering mausoleum is nearby. Go behind Chrysler's grave and you will see a chain-link fence. It is here that you can peer through the trees and possibly see, in the distance, the simple graves of Nelson Rockefeller and other family members buried at their private estate (which borders this cemetery).

The Ludlow Massacre happened at the Rockefeller-owned Colorado Fuel and Iron Mine in Ludlow, Colorado. In 1914, nine thousand miners struck the company for better working conditions. (Miners complained that the work mules were given better conditions than the men. Some reported that after the many mine collapses at the camp, the first thing the foremen would shout to the soot-covered survivors was, "Did the mules get out?") The miners formed large tent towns where they and their families retreated and lived during the work stoppage. The Rockefellers eventually turned the affair over to the Colorado State Militia. On April 20, 1914, "the bloodiest assault on organized labor in American history" took place. After the beatings and the shootings were ended, the toll was taken. More than twenty of the tent-dwellers were killed. In one instance, two women took eleven young children into a cellar out of harm's way. The militia burned the tents down, and the cellar too. They all died. Ludlow is a ghost town today. In nearby Trinidad, Colorado, where the victims were buried, stands a tall monument with their names and ages on it. Six of the children were under five years of age.

SAMUEL LANGHORNE CLEMENS _____

"Mark Twain"

Of all of the incongruities of this book, none is more striking than the circumstances of Mark Twain's final resting place. Why on earth would this great chronicler of the Mississippi, this voyager to the four corners of the world, this bon vivant and social gadfly, this friend of presidents and millionaires, be buried (of all places) in nondescript Elmira in New York's far-western Southern Tier? Actually, the reason is quite simple; his wife's family was from Elmira. But it still gives one a start to come upon the tall grave marker in this old military cemetery and see the name "MARK TWAIN" emblazoned on the top of the towering stone.

As a young man, Clemens lived all along the fertile banks of the mighty Mississippi in small towns like Hannibal, Missouri. From ages four to eighteen, he lived a life of ease and wonderment, caught up in the fascinating hustle and bustle of riverfront America. At twelve, his father died, and he had to quit school and go to work as a journeyman printer to help support his mother and siblings. He eventually found himself in St. Louis, Philadelphia, New Orleans, and then back in the Midwest. In his early twenties, he took an apprenticeship aboard a riverboat heading north from New Orleans on the Mississippi. He stayed in this job until the Civil War closed the river. He called his years as a boat captain his "university" and would always say that from that time on his "mistress was that old river."

A natural writer and storyteller, Clemens left the river at the beginning of the Civil War and started following his wanderlust. From Missouri to Nevada and eventually Virginia City, he traveled, observed, and wrote down his thoughts. In Virginia, he was hired as a newspaper journalist, and it was there that he took his pen name, Mark Twain, which is a river call for a depth of two fathoms. The paper featured Twain's much-told stories, and the public enjoyed them immensely.

He published his first book, *The Celebrated Jumping Frog of Calaveras County*, in 1867, and with its immediate success, other books soon followed. Perhaps his three greatest works all sprang from the memories of his riverfront childhood. *Life on the Mississippi, The Adventures of Tom Sawyer*, and *The Adventures of Huckleberry Finn* all brought him national fame and his first taste of personal wealth. The books charmed the reading public with warm morality tales of times gone by, of places familiar and comfortable, and of people drawn from real-life encounters. In fact, the characters in *Tom Sawyer* were almost all drawn from Twain's actual family. The judge was modeled after his father, Aunt Polly was a tribute to his mother, Big Jim was a real neighbor slave named Uncle Dan, and Tom Sawyer was a reflection of Twain himself as a young boy. His following books stretched Twain's imagination even further, encompassing Merry Olde England and Elizabethan tales of whimsy and mystery (*The Prince and the Pauper* and *A Connecticut Yankee in King Arthur's Court*).

Now heralded as one of America's foremost writers and humorists, he expanded his horizons to the business world. He opened his own publishing company in 1884 (The Charles L. Webster Company, named after a favorite nephew) and published several books, including his own. His initial publication, a mass printing of *Huck Finn*, sold more than 30,000 copies. His biggest coup came when former president Ulysses S. Grant was signed to write his memoirs for Twain's company. Grant, broke and in precarious health, worked hand in hand with the publisher in completing the massive book, and in fact finished his *Memoirs* just days before dying. The book sold over 100,000 copies, and the royalty check paid to Grant's widow, $500,000, was at the time the largest ever awarded in American publishing history.

Sensing a hunger in the reading public to learn more about the recently ended Civil War, Twain contracted many of the war's great generals to write their autobiographies. It was a major miscalculation. While the public couldn't get enough of the tales of the victorious Union leader Grant, the war stories of the lesser generals (McClellan, Sheridan, Sherman, etc.) found few takers. Unsold books filled Twain's warehouses and eventually drove him to bankruptcy. On February 1, 1886, he filed for protection from his creditors.

America was shocked at the financial bad news befalling one of its most beloved authors. A front-page story in the *New York Herald* newspaper pleaded for "Dollars For Twain." Contributions poured in. Andrew Carnegie pledged $1,000 towards Twain's financial relief; Broadway producer Charles Frohman gave $100; financier Joseph Guggenheim pledged $100; and a group identified only as "The Brooklynites" gave a sum of $1. In short time, Twain was solvent.

As a writer, Twain was clever, thoughtful, and brilliant. As a businessman, he was none of these. A lover of inventions, he never met a gadget he didn't like. In fact, Twain held three U.S. Patents of his own—one for an adjustable shirt strap, one for a memory-building game, and one for a glue-less scrapbook. None made him rich. After losing more than $100,000 in a typesetting machine investment, he finally gave up his quest for the "golden egg" and stuck with writing.

Twain became one of America's most colorful celebrities and drew huge crowds wherever he was engaged. He embarked on a lecture tour around the world and appeared in front of standing-room-only crowds everywhere. He hobnobbed with Rockefellers and Carnegies and received honors from Oxford and Yale.

When a favorite daughter, Susy, died in 1896, some say Twain's writing brilliance dimmed. In 1904, his beautiful wife of thirty-five years, Livy, died, and on Christmas Eve of 1909, another daughter, Jean, drowned in a bathtub. Observers commented that Twain was greatly diminished proportionately by each tragic loss.

His last years were spent living in one or another of the several lavish homes he had built. During his prime, he owned mansions in the Hudson Valley, Connecticut, and London, England. He also had a sprawling summer home, "Quarry Farm," in Elmira and a historic three-story home in New York's Greenwich Village.

He died peacefully on April 21, 1910. He had been reading in bed (Carlyles' *French Revolution*), and his final words were to a nurse, "Please give me my reading glasses."

Twain is buried with his wife's family (to which he had grown extremely close). After a large funeral in New York City, which thousands attended, he was buried at Woodlawn Cemetery in Elmira. A tall monument in Section G marks his final resting place (carrying both his given and taken names). A striking profile of the author adorns the front of the marker. It is odd to note that there are two names and profiles on Clemens' memorial obelisk. The other visage belongs to Ossip Gabrilowitsch, Twain's son-in-law, who was a world famous pianist and conductor of the Detroit Symphony. Ossip and Clara Clemens Gabrilowitsch are also both buried in this family plot.

Author's note: Woodlawn Cemetery is an important cemetery from a historical point of view. On the northeastern edge is a section known as National Cemetery. Here are interred the remains of more than three thousand *Confederate* soldiers who died in a nearby Civil War prison camp. It is a sad footnote that so many thousands of Americans from the South are buried so far from their homes.

Other famous names buried at Woodlawn are Heisman Trophy winner Ernie Davis (see his entry in this book), former New York Governor Lucius Robinson (Section A), and Hal Roach, famed Hollywood pioneer and creator of *The Little Rascals*.

Woodlawn is located at 1200 Walnut Street in Elmira. The city is full of Mark Twain historical sites including the exquisite Quarry Farm, where he lived for twenty years and wrote *Tom Sawyer*, *Prince and the Pauper*, *Huck Finn*, and *Connecticut Yankee*. His original writing study has been moved to nearby Elmira College. It is open daily from mid-June to Labor Day. For information about these two sites, call 607-735-1941. Elmira even boasts a Mark Twain Golf Course! Other famous landmarks concerning Twain can be found in Hartford, Connecticut, where he lived from 1874 to 1891 (The Mark Twain House, 351 Farmingham Avenue, Hartford). A new fifteen-million-dollar visitor center and museum opened in 2002 (www.marktwain.org). Twain's boyhood home in Hannibal, Missouri, is also a much-visited historic site. In "Frogtown, California," a reconstructed "Angel's Camp" can be visited. This is where Twain first heard the celebrated "jumping frog" story in 1863. The Mark Twain National Forest runs throughout central Missouri, near Rulla (573-364-4621).

DANIEL BISSELL

"The First Purple Heart"

The U.S. Army officially listed Daniel Bissell as a deserter. General Washington ordered this so as to mask Bissell's real identity and purpose, "Master Spy" for Washington's troops!

In 1791, the young Bissell walked away from the American Army and fled to New York City. There, for the next thirteen months, he played the role of a discontented deserter preparing to join up with the British Army. He was so convincing in this part that he was able to ascertain vital information about the enemy and their troop strengths and deployment. He observed sensitive British maps and listened in on key strategy sessions between enemy officers. At the completion of his duty, he fled back to General Washington to report on what he learned. But Dan Bissell's mission was far from over.

Along his escape route back to headquarters, he became seriously ill and was taken to a British hospital. There, for weeks hovering between life and death, his fever caused him to babble incoherently for days on end. Seemingly out of his mind with delirium, Bissell had no way of knowing that he had blurted out all of the information that he was secreting out. The British doctor either took his rantings as the ravings of a madman or chose to sympathetically ignore what he heard. In any case, after a month of recuperation, Bissell was able to continue his escape and returned to General Washington with his vital reports.

For his bravery and meritorious conduct, he was awarded the newly commissioned Award of Merit (Purple Heart) in 1783, one of only three so honored at that time.

Daniel Bissell is buried in the Episcopalian cemetery in Allen's Hill, New York.

Author's note: Allen's Hill is one of the smallest communities where an Upstate New York legend in this book lies. It is actually a remote, rural crossroads located high in the Finger Lakes region. It lies midway between Honeoye Lake and NYS Route 20 on County Route 40, at Belcher Road. It is approximately ten miles south of the town of Bloomfield. From the Allen's Hill Cemetery (one of the only landmarks of this crossroads locale), you can see the beautiful shores of Honeoye Lake and the gently rolling foothills of western New York.

The inscription on Dan Bissell's gravestone reads, "In memory of Daniel Bissell, who died August 21, 1824. Aged 70 years. He had the confidence of Washington, from whom he received a Badge of Merit." It should be noted that General Washington awarded only *three* Purple Hearts in 1783. The other two original recipients were Sgts. William Brown and Elijah Churchill. (Some newly discovered information points to Sgt. Churchill as being the actual first recipient of the three, which would make Sgt. Bissell, at the very least, New York State's first Purple Heart winner. All three soldiers were from western Connecticut, with only Bissell having lived, and ultimately, been buried in New York State.) There are two known original Purple Heart medals in existence. One is in Washington, D.C., and the other is located at General George Washington's Headquarters State Historical Park in Newburgh, New York. The original award (called the Award of Merit and created and designed by Washington himself) is described this way: "Attached to a piece of dark blue cloth is a purple heart made of silk, bound with braid and edged in lace." The blue cloth is believed to be an original piece of fabric from the tunic or uniform of a Continental Army soldier. The Headquarters State Park historic site (the *first* state historical site in America) is located at the corner of Liberty and Washington Streets, Newburgh, New York. Many activities and exhibits are planned yearly. For more information, phone 845-562-1195.

ONE FOR THE ROAD ...

"The Split-Elm Grave of Catherine Vanderbogart"

Over the past ten years or so, my travels have taken me to every corner of New York State, chasing down leads on the final resting places of many American legends. One of the most bizarre and memorable finds was the grave of young Catherine Vanderbogart in Woodstock, New York.

Catherine was a beautiful girl still in her teens in 1820 when she married John Vanderbogart, a rough citizen of Woodstock with a questionable past. He was far older than his young bride, and soon after their wedding, their relationship turned into a troublesome affair. John was a drunk who would often become violent after too many tankards of ale, and usually poor Catherine was the object of his inebriated fury.

One night, when Catherine was eight months pregnant with their first child, she decided to go and visit a nearby neighbor for some companionship. John had been on a binge for days and had been home only infrequently. The rule laid down by the man of the house was that Catherine was to *never* leave home at night, especially if John was not there. When he came home to an empty house this night, he flew into a rage. He imagined that his young wife was surely meeting some younger paramour, and jealousy fueled his ire. He was determined to teach Catherine a lesson she would never forget when she arrived home.

He went into the back yard of their home and ripped a large elm branch from a tree. He returned to the house and stood waiting in the dark for her to return. When Catherine entered the front door from her innocent visit with her neighbor, John set upon her furiously, beating her severely with the elm branch.

As Catherine lay bleeding on the kitchen floor, John came to his senses and, realizing the viciousness of his act, held her and begged for forgiveness. By now, the commotion from the Vanderbogart home had wakened half the town, and a crowd gathered out front. A constable was summoned. When the officer asked poor Catherine who had beaten her so savagely, she whimpered that it had been so dark that she was unable to identify her attacker. A doctor was called to the home where, after a thorough examination, John was told that neither his bride nor his child would survive the night. They carried Catherine to her bedroom for her last night on earth.

In the early morning hours of the next day, Catherine awoke with a start from her coma-like sleep and called for her husband. She pulled John's face close to hers and whispered, "John, I know it was you who beat me. You can't deny it to me. My last request before I die is that you bury me alongside the elm branch which you raised against me in anger. That way when you visit my grave you will always remember what you did to me and what you did to our child." In tears, John agreed to her last request. Catherine died an hour later.

John buried his wife and child in the center section of the old rural cemetery on the edge of Woodstock, New York. Seized with remorse and grief, he buried the elm branch inside the coffin with Catherine as she wished.

Week after week, old John would traipse out to the cemetery to mourn his loss. He was a pathetic and solitary sight at the cemetery at all times of day and night. He stopped drinking and dedicated the rest of his life to the memory of his wife. One day, while visiting her grave, he noticed a twig sprouting out from under the headstone. In a week or so, it grew to a small bush. John believed it was the elm branch growing out of Catherine's grave. He pulled the bush out of the dirt with his bare hands, but it sprouted anew within days. In a frenzy, he did everything in his power to keep this demonic reminder of his terrible deed from reappearing. Each time he tried to eliminate the branch, it would grow back more determined than ever to flourish.

John went half mad trying to kill this living reminder of what he did to Catherine. One day, after an absence of several weeks, John returned to the gravesite and was astounded to see that the elm branch had grown out of the earth, up through the stone marker, and had actually split the stone into two pieces! The bottom part of the slab was now in front and the top half (bearing Catherine's name and birth date) jutted out from the ground behind it. Knowing this was a message of revenge from his departed spouse, John Vanderbogart began drinking heavily again and slowly disappeared into an insane oblivion.

"The Split-Elm Grave of Catherine Vanderbogart" is one of the truly great legends of the Catskill Mountains. And even though the story has been told for almost two centuries, nobody *really* knows if it is true, apocryphal, or merely folklore at its best. Tall tale or not, one thing is for sure … Catherine's grave is still there and is still split in two!

Author's note: Woodstock, New York, in the heart of the Catskill Mountains, is famous for its homespun shops and mountain vistas. Old Woodstock Cemetery is merely three blocks away from the hurly-burly of the town square. Catherine's grave is located in the center, straight back from the driveway leading into the cemetery. And, yes, a tall elm tree still grows out between the two slabs of the gravestone! Although the marker is very disfigured with age, a close examination will still reveal these words on the stone: "Here lies Catherine Vanderbogart, wife of John Vanderbogart, and her infant child who died on August 2, 1821 at the age of eighteen."

And Last But Not Least ..._____

WILLIAM McCONKEY
"The Man with the Boat
(But What a Boat It Was!)"

It was just a matter of being in the right place at the right time. Of all of the entries in *Great Graves*, from the movie stars to the millionaires, the one gravesite that has intrigued me the most is the grave of one William McConkey. He was a ferry owner who had a small boatyard and inn on the Delaware River at the spot George Washington chose to make his historic crossing for his daring Christmas raid on the Hessians' encampment at Trenton.

Washington, seeking to strike a much-needed blow to the enemy, chose the early morning hours of the day after Christmas, 1776, to make his move. With the enemy still groggy from the all-night reverie, Washington mustered his master boatmen, under the charge of Col. John Glover, for a strike into the heart of the enemy camp. The weather was frightful with strong gusty winds blowing across the flat plain of the frozen Delaware River. The temperature hovered around zero. General Washington ordered boats to be moved to McConkey's ferry crossing. Sixteen Durham boats and flats, usually used to ferry cargo and livestock across the river, were procured. The owner of the longboat that Washington picked as his rickety "flagship" was a soldier named William McConkey. Despite treacherous conditions, McConkey saw to it that the general got to the distant shore safely, where Washington then led his troops to a surprise victory over the much larger force. In fact, nearly the entire enemy force was either killed or captured by the colonists. It is unknown whether McConkey was actually *in* the same boat as Washington, but speculation has it that he was. If he did accompany the general on his trip across the Delaware, you can be assured that Emanuel Leutze, the painter who so famously captured *Washington Crossing the Delaware*, would have surely put the Scotsman McConkey squarely at the rudder!

I literally stumbled upon the gravesite of this unsung patriot while on a "cemetery ride" one day. While traveling north on Route 30A, heading from Cobleskill to Amsterdam (New York), just up the road from the beautiful Schoharie Valley, I caught a glimmer of something shiny in the weeds along the road and stopped to explore. It was the overgrown (but freshly painted) New York State historical marker denoting the gravesite of William McConkey. The area was seriously overgrown with brush and debris, but I stoically entered the small field to discover more. There, just a few hundred feet off the side of this busy road I found an old, forgotten cemetery holding the remains of less than two dozen people. Two of the headstones are from the Revolutionary War era, making this a remarkable spot. McConkey's ancient stone is weatherworn and in disrepair, but still easily identifiable. The exact location of this resting place is one mile south of the Town of Charleston on the west side of Route 30A.

McConkey's original ferry and inn are still intact and are part of the Washington Crossing National Historical Park. Tours are available and many visitors come to Washington Crossing, Pennsylvania, every year (215-493-4076) to see these and other Revolutionary War sites.

And so, even though he was just a man with a boat, William McConkey was certainly the right man with the right boat at the right time in American history and is therefore included in *Great Graves*.

Author's Final Word _____

Some people might ask, "Why just seventy names in this book?" That is a question without an answer. I guess fifty would have seemed too "ordinary" and maybe one hundred would have seemed too much. So seventy it is! My journey to the cemeteries of Upstate New York is never really finished, though. There is nothing I like better, on a beautiful color-filled autumn day, than to wander the beauteous paths of an ancient rural cemetery. There is just so much history in the ordinariness of it all. And, yes, once in a while, a familiar name from the past will call to me. I keep my lists, I add new names, and I am always setting off on another great adventure to one of the far corners of my state. And I mean it when I say my search for famous names in cemeteries is never finished. And who knows, maybe you live in a community in Upstate New York where a legend lies unnoticed. If so, let me know, and I will certainly consider placing your entry in my next book.

—Chuck D'Imperio

(NewYorkGraves@aol.com)

ABOUT THE AUTHOR_____

Chuck D'Imperio is a longtime broadcaster at WDOS/WSRK Radio in Central New York. He has been a contributing writer for national and state magazines and for the Gannett News Corporation. Chuck has had a long love of history and New York State folklore and has been researching the graves of the famous in New York for more than a decade. His popular articles, titled "Where Legends Lie," were featured in New York Alive and Kaatskill Life magazines for years. He also is the author of a popular two-volume edition of memories of growing up in small-town America: *My Town is a Cathedral* (www.SidneyNewYorkBook.com). He was inducted into the New York State Country Music Hall of Fame as "Broadcaster of the Year" in 2000. He is a bona fide 1977 winner of the classic TV program The Gong Show, receiving a perfect score for his powerful and touching rendition of "Bad, Bad LeRoy Brown" while singing naked in a shower on national television! He and his wife, Trish, reside in Oneonta, New York. They are the parents of Frances, Katie, Abby, and Joey. They also are the owners of CooperstownWalks!, giving guided walking tours of historic Cooperstown, New York (www.CooperstownWalks.com).